BEYOND
SECOND CHANCES
Heartbreak to Joy

BEYOND
SECOND CHANCES

Heartbreak to Joy

SHIRLEY QUIRING MOZENA

Published by Second Chances Ministry (www.shirleymozena.com)

ISBN Paperback: 979-8-9891355-2-3
ISBN Ebook: 979-8-9891355-3-0

Library of Congress Catalog Card Number: 2023919440

DEDICATION

This book is dedicated to my husband, Jim, who stirred me to write this book. On our refrigerator is a white board with a hand written statement. It says: *Once upon a time, God brought Jim and Shirley together…and they lived happily ever after.* The statement is so true, for God did bring us together, and we will live happily ever after—with our Lord and Savior, Jesus Christ in Heaven! Our time on earth is up to the Maker of the Universe. He knows our days and we rest in that. He can be trusted.

Jim listened to my stories and asked the questions. And I am grateful. I love you, James Patrick Mozena! You brought joy into my life once again.

CONTENTS

ACKNOWLEDGEMENTS

My story would be hollow and just another memoir without God's redemption story. I am so grateful to my loving Savior, who was there during the dark times and and joyful times, too.

I am thankful to my parents, Henry and Rose Quiring who followed Jesus Christ and passed on their love of Him to each of their children.

Without my siblings, there'd be no stories. God bless you: Joyce, Roger, Eileen, and Betsy. Our past belongs to us.

I am grateful for my editors, Christi Krug, Danica Swiggers, and Joyce Erickson. Thank you.

The five of us recently (Pictured L-R in their birth order: Joyce, Roger, Shirley, Eileen, Betsy).

CHAPTER 1

THE WEDDING IS OFF

"Their strength is to sit still."
—Isaiah 30:7

"I can't do this," he said.

"Do what?"

"Marry you."

My stomach plummeted. My heart raced as I gulped air. My hands shook.

We were talking on the phone, just as we did every evening before Ron went to bed. He would wear sweats and relax in his favorite recliner while I would curl up on my couch, imagining him beside me.

His voice always got to me. It was a deep baritone with a sexy twist to it. I could see him sitting with his head back, taking his wire-framed glasses off and rubbing the ridge of his nose as he thought and talked. He lived more than two hundred miles away—but we would be together soon.

"What?" I asked. *Had I heard him correctly?*

There had been no indication that something was wrong. We'd sent loving text messages to each other all day. Just that weekend, we'd gone through Ron's home to decide what we'd keep, sell, or give away. I'd put earnest money down on a house we were buying together. The wedding was in five weeks. We loved each other—or so I thought.

Our engagement had been tumultuous. My daughter hadn't approved. "Mom. He isn't your type. You can do better. It's too soon since you've met."

"It's no sooner than when Blair asked me," I countered. "What's wrong with him? He's a Christian. He loves me."

"What's the hurry?" she asked, frustrated. "I think you're desperate to be married."

"I am *not* desperate!" I said hotly.

My family and their opinions were important to me. But I stubbornly thought Ron was a fine man. We shared our faith. His politics were similar to mine. He loved his kids.

But there were red flags. His sister, Stephanie said, "Ron just can't be happy—I don't know why. He's impulsive!"

Once, after purchasing a motorcycle and realizing it was too expensive for his budget, he rode it to the dealership, parked it in the lot, and left without making another payment.

His past relationships had been rocky and he'd been married several times. *That's before he met Christ, though,* I thought.

Small voices clamored for my attention. *This feels wrong. Should I be the only one putting money down on the house? Shouldn't we be sharing the earnest money agreement?*

Yet I had ignored all the signs.

"I think we need to put the marriage on hold," Ron continued as my mind reeled. Numb, I hung up the phone.

A verse from my early morning devotions drifted into my mind. *He does great things past finding out. Yes, wonders without wonder.*[1]

I knew my Savior had done great things in my life. He'd been there during the hard times. Two years earlier, after only seventeen months of marriage, my second husband Blair had died of a brain aneurysm.

But life was better now, wasn't it? I was engaged to be married! Soon I wouldn't be alone anymore.

That morning I had begun my prayers, lifting up my children and plans for the day. As I closed my prayer, I uttered words that surprised me. "Oh God, I don't have the strength to do it, but if this marriage is out of Your will, then *You* will have to end it." I was mystified by my words but didn't think much about it. After all, Ron and I had prayed regularly for God's will regarding our relationship.

It was strange, the rush of emotions that flooded me that night after the call. I was embarrassed and hurt by the rejection. This pain was different than the deaths of Bill and Blair. I was angry at Ron. Why didn't he want me? These feelings reflected a disturbing part of my personality I didn't like. There was pride gleaming back there and it wasn't pretty! Yet beyond the feelings of rejection, I also felt relieved.

As I lay in bed that night, I reflected. *The house—I put money down. The financing is nearly done. They're going to appraise it in a few days.* Even though Ron said we should not talk for a week, I needed to know whether to call the realtor. I slept fitfully that night.

Next morning I texted him. *Should I call off buying the house?* After twenty minutes, he responded with one word.

Yes.

In a panic, I rang his number. When he answered, his voice was cold and distant. The engagement was over.

The realtor informed me it might be one day too late to call off the sale. Unless the seller agreed to forgive the cancellation, I'd lose my five grand. I didn't want to buy the house if we were not going to get married. *Ron will have to help with the loss of money,* I thought.

I visited my pastor, Brian. It was a busy afternoon with many preparations for Good Friday and Easter. Pastor Brian sat back in his chair and took a sip of coffee, glancing at the photo of his young family in front of him. I knew he cared about me by the way he spoke, gazing into my eyes carefully and respectfully.

"Shirley, this is not a surprise to God," he said with a serious expression on his face. "It's the best way."

In my heart, I knew he was right. I called my family, who were as shocked as I was about the wedding cancellation. Their faces seemed relieved—and yet they told me how much they cared. They felt my pain.

I needed space to pray and think. I decided on a weekend trip. Nestled in the Willamette Valley, the Oregon Gardens offered lovely accommodations and a quiet place to stay.

My stomach churned as I drove through the winding roads toward my destination. With each curve in the road, a beautiful spring scene attempted to capture my attention. I wanted to drive to Ron's home and beg him to change his mind. I longed for his arms around me but I was angry at him for breaking our engagement on the phone instead of face-to-face. I was wounded and wanted to strike out.

As I walked among the early spring gardens, new beginnings of growth showed in the bare, brown palette of the grounds. My heart felt barren. The early pink cherry blossoms glowed against the dark trunks and reached up to the blue sky, studded with wispy white clouds. The ponds were coming to life with new grasses growing among the dead cattails and thistle. I listened to the birds singing.

Awareness flooded me: I was alone. I hated it! I strolled through the grounds and admired the arrogant, yellow daffodils with their large trumpets, as if declaring a joyous sound in color. Nearby, their jonquil cousins with white-collar petals and orange snub noses seemed to say, "We're important too." There were house-sized flower boxes holding bare trees. Yellow and white primroses grew on the ground beneath, seeming to smile in the spring sunlight. After all of these lovely images, I turned to the friendly faces of the purple and yellow pansies. My heart lifted. I knew I would be okay.

I walked slowly back to my room, where a king-sized bed nearly filled the space, covered with a cozy white comforter and a darker green shawl at the foot. I turned on the gas fireplace, opened the French doors onto my secluded deck, and sat at the table to compose a letter.

> Dear Ron,
>   I've been thinking for two days now and I think I can write it without too much sharpness.
> I will miss your gestures of love.
>   You left a mess for me to clean up—but that's nothing like the mess you made of my heart, Ron. That will take a little more time.
>   I will be okay, though. For I know about loss. I'm glad you showed me who you really are. It is better this way.

I felt better after I wrote the letter. *It sounds bitter,* I thought. Even so, I recopied it and sent it to his email address.

I decided to treat myself to a dinner date. *Alone, but not lonely.* I dressed up in my new cream skirt with a ruffled, sleeveless peach blouse. Shimmering stockings graced my legs and strappy, satin cream heels completed my outfit. I had bought those shoes and stockings to wear on my wedding day. *I'll wear them now,* I thought.

"You look lovely," the maitre'd said as he seated me. I thanked him and glanced around the room. An elderly couple nearby had nearly finished dinner. The gentleman was dressed in khaki slacks with a natty navy blazer. She was wearing a silk green pantsuit with a pink rose corsage pinned to her left lapel. She seemed to have a debilitating muscular disease when she scooted toward the edge of the booth. Her tall, slightly stooping husband helped her rise from the elevated seating area. There was a little struggle as she attempted to slide from her seat and support herself on the three-footed cane her husband was holding. She glanced over at me and our eyes met.

"Enjoy your youth!" she joked.

"I'm not that far behind you," I retorted, smiling. We chuckled together and I bid them a good evening.

A server came to my table, sporting a neatly tied white apron and a Marine Corps tattoo peeking above his white dress shirt. "Would you like something to drink?"

Why not? I was treating myself! "What about this Moonstone Martini?"

I waited for my treat and watched another couple sharing a dessert. I wondered what they were celebrating—an anniversary? Or perhaps the Easter weekend. Again I realized I was alone. I felt a stab of pain. I didn't like it at all.

The server brought my ruby-red drink in a martini glass and I began to sip with anticipation. I was astounded by the fermented fruity bitterness. It reminded me of cough syrup and I felt a wave of irritation. Why hadn't I stuck with a Lemon Drop, or a glass of good wine?

The penne pasta with spinach and roasted garlic was passable. Most likely it was my attitude and not the chef's creation that left me unsatisfied with my meal. I sighed, tossed my napkin on the table, and walked back to my room. As I walked through the door I pulled off the shoes that were pinching my toes. *So much for wearing those while standing.* "They're killing my feet," I said softly to the empty room.

I knew the night would be long but I was prepared for it. I opened my Bible to Habakkuk 2:1.

> I will stand at my watch and station myself on the ramparts; I will look to see what he will say to me.

As I prayed, I felt myself wanting an answer immediately.

I read a little of Hannah Whitall Smith,[2] a writer from more than one hundred years ago. She had struggled in a situation where there was nothing to be done but sit still and wait. I realized I needed to wait, too.

I thought back again to the prayer I had said three days earlier: "Oh God, I don't have the strength to do it, but if this marriage is not in Your will, then *You* will have to end it." I had asked God for an answer—and He had given it.

I now needed to begin the task of forgiving Ron. God was using two imperfect people to do His will in their lives. I begged God to help me move forward, away from the planned marriage, toward peace and His future for me.

Perhaps I would never be married again. In any case, I needed to submit my will to God's. I set myself to the work of grief and forgiveness. I knew it would happen soon, even if I couldn't feel it yet. I surrendered all my thoughts to God, and just before dawn, I fell asleep.

When I woke later that morning, I was at peace. I was sad but grateful for the holy intervention so evident in my prayer earlier that week. I knew it was God's best for me—He *had* spoken to me through that prayer, said not by me but by the Holy Spirit living in me. Though I was hurt, I knew my heart would heal—if I allowed the Comforter to help.

Later that day, I drove home and began adjusting my life back to what it had been before I met Ron. This experience was different from losing a loved one to death. The wrenching feelings of loss and abandonment were different. In this break-up, I was angry—I was angry at Ron.

CHAPTER 2

MOVING FORWARD— AGAIN!

"Every good and perfect gift is from above, coming
down from the Father of the heavenly lights, who
does not change like shifting shadows."
—James 1:17

It was just before meeting Ron that I'd thought I might be ready to
date and marry again. Yet all my hopes had left me with nothing
but a deficit of $5,000 earnest money. Here I was again—alone.

"Should we go to dinner tonight?" asked my best friend, Connie.

"I have my computer class downtown. Why don't you come
with me and we'll go after?"

Connie wandered through Portland's Pioneer Square while I had
my technology session. I was learning how to use my new iMac.

Blair and I had lost our laptop's hard drive and I'd gotten this
new computer. It had been nearly two years since my husband had
entered his eternal home in heaven.

Connie and I strolled among the busy Christmas shopping
crowds at Nordstrom. I found an iPad cover in the clearance bin.
"Look, Connie! What do you think about this?" I showed her my
find: a shiny, rich burgundy. She smiled and nodded.

I needed help to make purchasing decisions. Connie helped—
especially in the two years since Blair had died. Earlier, she had
urged me to buy a comforter set in the soft rose and creamy beige
that made me happy. The year before, she and her daughter Alex
had trotted different outfits into my fitting room for me to try on
before a trip.

One thing I'd never done alone was buy a car. Before marriage, I used the family Chevrolet—if I could get it—for driving to work and school. When I was nineteen, I married Bill and we owned a dark green MG Midget roadster, plus an old Studebaker for when the better car was in use. The Studebaker was a four-door sedan with doors that wouldn't stay shut. Bill tied a rope from one door's armrest to an opposite armrest in the backseat to keep them closed. It was okay, though—we were students and we didn't care how that second car looked.

When the day finally came to buy a new car, Bill and I sat at the table with the salesman. Bill did the negotiating. "I won't buy it unless this is included," he said firmly, sliding the paper with an offer across the table. I supported him silently and soon, with the agreed price, we were the owners of a brand new 1991 Subaru Loyale Wagon.

We enjoyed that car on backpacking trips and climbing adventures for years to come. Later, when Blair and I married, we decided to name our cars. My red Jetta was German, so we named it Fritz. Blair's was a Japanese van we called Samurai. "I'm taking Fritz" seemed much friendlier than "I'm taking *my* car."

Now Fritz was becoming needy, requiring new parts. It was time to get a new car and it was scary, doing it on my own. I talked it over with my son Todd and we narrowed it down to three different models.

I bravely walked into the dealership and a friendly salesman helped me. "If you bought a car today, what color would you like?" he asked.

"Red, just like my old car," I said firmly.

The salesman and I took a car out on a test drive. We sat down at the negotiating table to discuss financing options and warranties. My son was there to support me via cell phone set on speaker. We negotiated a price and, later that day, I drove off the lot with my red Volkswagen Jetta. I was excited and proud.

Shirley with her first car purchase.

Now, in Pioneer Square with Connie, she announced, "I'm starved! Let's go to dinner."

We found a table at the Macaroni Grill, busy with Christmas shoppers. Our window looked out on the street, shiny from a recent rain shower. Bright red and green lights from holiday decorations reflected brightly on the wet pavement.

A couple stood arm in arm, chatting together. A young mother was pushing a stroller with one hand while holding her three-year-old with the other. Three teenagers waited for the Max light rail train. Each had a cell phone in hand, texting some unknown person, ignoring their friends nearby.

I don't feel sad tonight, I thought.

Instead of mourning my loss, I was interested in people's faces. I wondered about their conversations. I didn't carry the heaviness that had accompanied my losses for so long—I felt alive.

I had read a number of books including *Getting to the Other Side of Grief,*[3] which showed me that grieving is like a journey on a

21

road. There are roadblocks along the way and I would have to wait for them to clear in order to move on. I might encounter a traffic jam of grief when I could do nothing but wait on the memories and sadness, forced to move at a slower pace. But finally the road would clear and I would emerge on the other side.

I liked the promise that there would be another side. I didn't want to be grieving for the rest of my life. At the same time, I began to understand that getting to "the other side" didn't mean forgetting the precious memories embedded in my heart. I could build memories that didn't include my late spouses, creating a new history apart from my loved ones. In this way, "moving forward" was different from "moving on."

Reflections of a Grieving Spouse[4] was another book that helped me. I realized that there are often no answers to our questions of grief. Even if we do know the answers, they don't change reality. Ultimately, we must depend on and trust in God. We need to remember who we are and who God is. Author Norman Wright asks, "Could it possibly be that within the 'no answer' there exists the mercy and comfort of God? Yes. He knows what we can know, what we can understand, and what we can handle."

Among my other books, some helped more, some less. But in all of my study, I read and reflected on the life I'd shared with my loved ones. I was hopeful that the pain would lessen one day and I would experience a joy moment.

And now with Connie, I seemed to be in that moment. Oh, I was grateful!

We dipped rosemary bread in plates of olive oil and balsamic vinegar. "We're getting our tree tomorrow," Connie said, "but otherwise, I'm ready for Christmas." Though I still missed my dear Blair and dreaded the thought of a holiday without him, I felt my heart lighten as we chatted. That evening gave me a glimpse of perhaps more joy to come.

In early December, sitting in my pastor's office one day, Pastor Paul listened to me pour out my heart about my loneliness and my desire to be married again. "If you marry the wrong person, Shirley, it will renew your grief for Blair," he said. "The wrong person could say something hurtful and you might think, 'Blair wouldn't do that!' Finding another person like you did with Blair is highly unlikely. I've sat at my desk many times and have heard from people who have *not* had such a relationship. Add the fact that you've had *two* husbands who loved you, and you will see that you've been very blessed."

I knew he was right, but I hated being alone! I couldn't even stand to say I was a "widow"—a word used to describe a certain spider.

"Why can't it happen again?" I countered.

"It can, but it's not likely. Can you face life without a husband?"

"I—I guess so."

I began to experience even more joy moments in my life. I also learned that I *could* do things on my own. But as I reflected on my conversation with Pastor Paul, my stubbornness began to rear its head once again. I wanted to prove him wrong!

CHAPTER 3

LIFE ALONE

"He defends the cause of the fatherless and the
widow . . . giving [them] food and clothing."
—Deuteronomy 10:18

"Isn't that an eagle?" I exclaimed, looking up at the sky in front
of my house.

"I've noticed him circling around your house all day," remarked
my neighbor as she walked by my home. Linda was the consummate
walker in the neighborhood and spent hours outside. If she noticed
the eagle's presence, I believed it to be true.

It had been one week since Bill, my husband of forty years, had
died. For his memorial service, we had chosen to read Isaiah 40:31.

> But those who hope in the LORD will renew their strength. They
> will soar on wings like eagles; they will run and not grow weary,
> they will walk and not be faint.

At his graveside service, I noticed that a tall fir tree next to
Bill's grave held an eagle's nest. Now there was an eagle circling
our house—a place where none had been seen before. God was
showing me His care.

After the funeral, I went back to work in order to fill my time.
I repainted a living room, not knowing if my late husband would
have liked the colors I chose. I remodeled the bathrooms and the
entry hall, stripping wallpaper and making changes as I worked
through my aloneness. Afterwards, I would sleep well.

When it was time to update what had been our bedroom, I wanted it to be completely different. I gave away the queen-sized Sleep Number bed and used a travel poster's bright coral and yellow colors for design inspiration. I scavenged through garage sales and found bookshelves. I discovered a room screen with slots for photographs that I filled with pictures of family as well as a wedding shot of Bill and me. It was a comfort to see those smiling faces.

I found an antique bed frame. Now all I needed was a full-sized mattress set and the room would be complete.

One lunch break, I stumbled across a set for sale in the local classifieds. It was near my home and the cost was $175. I stopped by the bank to get the needed cash and made arrangements with the owner to stop by after work. *I'll offer them $150 and save a little bit,* I thought.

I found the home in the darkening evening. When I knocked on the door, a red-haired woman answered. She was around my age, in her fifties, and seemed to be home by herself. "Please have a seat." She gestured to the sofa nearby. "My name is Margie." I noticed a Bible sitting on the coffee table. *Maybe they're Christians,* I thought.

"We bought this set new for my husband's daughter. She's married now and we're making a quilting room that accommodates my quilting frame," she explained.

I shared with her my story about being a widow and the redecorating project I was working on. "I'm so sorry for your loss," Margie said. She told me she was a nurse and winced when I mentioned Bill's illness. We chatted some more and she mentioned that her husband worked nights. "When I put the ad in the newspaper, I prayed that a *woman* would want to buy the set. I was a little nervous about having someone come to the house at night while I'm home alone. I believe you're an answer to prayer! This was the last day of the ad and I didn't plan to run it again."

Wow! I thought. *I guess I'll give her full price. I can't offer her any less. This mattress is brand new.*

Before I could get the words out, she said, "I'd like to give you the mattress for a hundred and fifty. The Bible tells us to care for the widows and orphans."

"Thank you!" I was overwhelmed by her generosity.

"And by chance would you like this?" She held up a hand-crocheted pink afghan.

"Sure!"

I arranged to pick up the set the following Saturday and prepared to leave, the stack of bedding in my arms. With the afghan obscuring my vision, I lost my balance and stumbled as I left the porch, wrenching my knee. "Oh, dear. Are you all right?" Margie asked, concern in her voice.

"I—I think so." I picked myself up, a little embarrassed. My knee was throbbing and I hoped I'd be okay. I drove home and doctored myself with ice and prayer. "Oh, Lord, please don't let this fall do any real damage. I need to go to work tomorrow." I woke up the following morning with only slight stiffness in my knee. Another small miracle!

The following Saturday, I picked up the set with the help of a friend. "How's your knee?" Margie asked.

"I used lots of ice and ibuprofen and it seems fine," I told her.

"I'm so glad. I prayed all night for you. I felt so badly that you tripped and hurt yourself!"

I believe it was the prayers of this kind soul that enabled such a quick recovery.

I continued making changes. I gave our black Lab to our son. Bill had once said, "If anything happens to me, I want Todd to have Card." I was relieved I didn't have to take care of the dog and keep up his obedience training. It all seemed too much for me right then.

It was a difficult moment when I decided to sell Bill's truck to help me pay off the mortgage on my house.

"Every guy wants a truck, you know," Bill had often said. When we decided it was time to get his dream vehicle, Bill chose a 2004 Dodge Dakota in patriot blue. Bill added a canopy with side windows that swung out so he could access the entire truck bed. He added a liner, built stops for the dog kennel, and installed shelves for hunting supplies. After his death, I saw his special truck each time I walked into the garage.

The kennel remained in the back, no longer needed. I made arrangements to sell the truck and watched the new owner drive it away. There was a huge hole in the garage—and in my heart.

Life as a widow began to get easier. I had a new job at Columbia Machine, something totally different from my years of teaching elementary school. I found new energy. I began to take interest in yard landscaping projects. I went for walks in the neighborhood with my little dog, Poco. I was almost ready for new adventures.

CHAPTER 4

FINDING POCO

"A dog is the only thing on earth that loves
you more than he loves himself."
—Josh Billings

I thought back to the night Bill and I had spent at a benefit
auction for my school. Poco had come into my life as a cute
little Chihuahua puppy on the auction block.

The bidding began just after Bill and I finished a sumptuous
dinner. The bid sheet offered a week in a Puget Sound cottage, a
deep-sea fishing trip, a stay at a bed and breakfast in the mountains,
jewelry, and even monthly cheesecake delivery for a year. A teenage
girl in a purple lettermen sweater cuddled a tiny dog in her arms.
She threaded her way through the tables to display the dog to
potential bidders. As she stopped by each table, he shrank back
into her arms, frightened.

I'd never bid on anything and sat as still as possible. What if I
made an unexpected movement and the auctioneer thought I was
bidding?

After a flurry of bidding, the auctioneer asked the girl to hold
up the puppy. He was fawn-colored with white markings—it looked
like a can of white paint had spilled on top of his head and run
down both sides of his snout. "Here's a fine, full-breed Chihuahua
for that special dog lover. Do I hear a bid?"

Bill turned to me with a smile. "I think you need a dog," he
said. "What do you think?"

It was clear that Card really belonged to Bill. They worked hours each week together, retrieving ducks and geese. Bill even entered Card in hunting tests.

Still, I wasn't sure about getting another dog.

Then again, the puppy was darn cute. Out loud, I wondered if he'd fit in a backpack for a hike.

"I guess you could try," said Bill.

I heard a voice on the other side of the room. "Three hundred!"

"Do I hear three fifty?" the auctioneer asked.

Bill raised his hand. The auctioneer nodded in acknowledgement. "Do I hear three fifty-five?" It was quiet. "Going, going, gone for three-fifty!" The auctioneer slammed his gavel down with a clatter.

"You've got your own dog!" Bill declared. His full name in Spanish was *Cervato Poco* because of his resemblance to a deer fawn. To be honest, I wasn't that excited to train another puppy. But he caught on to our house rules quickly and Poco and I became the best of friends.

Now, two years later in my very quiet home, I was grateful for his presence.

That was, until . . .

Boom! The sound of firecrackers shook the air. Mortar shells and giant sparklers were released into the darkening sky. It was Fourth of July weekend, when city laws permitted a week of fireworks before and after the celebration day. The night sky was filled with colorful displays of light and sound. As always, it was great fun for the adults and kids, but animals feared the commotion and noise. Poco was one of them.

It had been five months since I had said my final goodbye to Bill. I had the bonus of a four-day weekend and decided that I'd paint my living and dining room. I'd been painting for hours, the doors flung open to disperse the strong smells. It was after eleven on that hot July night when Poco quietly wandered through the house.

I called for him, expecting to see the little dog with ears pointing straight up, curious about I wanted. I clapped my hands. "Come on, Poco-boy. Time for bed!" He didn't come when I whistled.

"Come on, Poco—come here!" I called again, with impatience in my voice. I walked outside and looked around. No dog. I threw up my hands, exhausted from a full day's work, and went to bed.

Morning came and Poco was still gone. I began to get concerned. I had a shopping trip planned but I left the back patio door open just in case he wandered back. When I returned in the late afternoon, Poco wasn't there. I started making lost dog posters. I shared the news with my two grandsons, seven-year-old Andrew and five-year-old Caleb, who prayed diligently that we would find him.

That evening, my family and friends joined me as we went door-to-door in pairs, asking if anyone had seen my little pooch. We walked several hours but did not find anyone who'd seen him.

While I was at work the next day, my daughter and her four children distributed posters farther away from my home.

A lump settled in my throat and I began to feel sorry for myself. *Why? Why do I have to suffer not only the loss of my husband, but my little companion and the playmate for my grandchildren?*

Since Card had been gone, Poco had been out of sorts. It had been amusing to watch the two dogs together; they were like brothers. Card had the typical good nature of his Labrador Retriever breed and was a calming influence on the feisty six-pound Chihuahua. If the doorbell rang, Card perked his ears up curiously before relaxing and putting his head down. In turn, the Chihuahua did not bark or yip as his breed normally would. Poco would simply back up next to Card, who lay flat on the floor, and place his hindquarters on the Lab's warm, shiny black back.

Now it seemed as though our prayers weren't being answered.

Little did we know, Poco was having his own adventure.

When I arrived home from work the next afternoon, I tossed my keys on the kitchen counter and noticed the answering machine was lit up.

"My name is Bob Johnson," played the message. "I think I know where your dog is. Call this number for more information." I quickly phoned, hoping he had my little companion.

After I asked several questions about Poco, Bob began a long story. "My wife and I were walking down Sixty-Third Avenue on

Friday evening when we noticed a big dog trying to fight with yours. We picked the little guy up and took him home with us. There was no tag so we kept him."

"I know he doesn't have a tag. I've been meaning to do that," I said regretfully.

Bob paused for a moment. "He didn't seem to be injured. Mostly scared." That sounded like Poco. He had the Chihuahua-bold heart but underneath the bravado was fear. "I'm a pyro-technician and I had a fireworks show at Neskowin—you know, the small coastal town—for their Fourth celebration. We didn't feel comfortable leaving your dog home alone, so we took him with us. When our fireworks show was over and we were ready to drive home, we realized Poco had run away!" Once again, the loud sounds and commotion had frightened Poco and off he went. "We tried to find him, but I had to get back to Vancouver to my job the next day. I felt terrible, leaving him there, but we didn't know what else to do." Now Poco was a hundred miles away from home!

He continued his story. "I called the mayor of the town and asked her to check the animal shelter for a lost dog. Sure enough, they found a Chihuahua wandering about a mile down from the fireworks site. It's a real miracle!"

"My grandsons and I have been praying that a miracle would happen and we would find him," I said, shaking my head in amazement.

"My wife is willing to make the drive to the beach, but we'd appreciate some help for the gas," he said hesitantly.

"Of course," I said, relieved I didn't have to take the time off and make the drive myself.

After work the next day, I walked over to the Johnsons' to pick up Poco. "He hasn't eaten anything. He must really miss you," Mrs. Johnson said.

Poco seemed aloof; wary of me. So many strangers had reached out to him that he was thoroughly confused and scared.

I cuddled him as I walked back to my house and put him down in the backyard where he slowly explored, sniffing. Soon he began running and barking joyfully. He trotted up to me and took a swipe at my cheek with his tongue. His fear had seemed to vanish. Poco was home—my little guy was back.

Poco's exploit was another reminder of the extra-special consideration we received from my Savior when my family truly needed it. And perhaps it was a way of preparing me for my own next adventure.

CHAPTER 5

BACK THERE AGAIN

"Those we hold most dear never truly leave us . . . They
live on in the kindnesses they showed, the comfort they
shared, and the love they brought into our lives."
—Isabel Norton

I was sitting in my morning room, bundled in the cozy pink
afghan. It was long before daylight but I couldn't sleep. Blair
had been gone only nineteen days.

As I held the steamy cup of coffee in my hand, reading
Scripture, I heard a thumping sound—like a cord blown by the
wind, slapping the side of the house. I tried to ignore it, but the
sound continued. I checked the front of the house and didn't see
anything. Again, I heard the thumping. I sighed and checked the
back of the house—nothing.

When the sound persisted, I got up again to check the garage.
As I walked by the powder room, I noticed a large red-breasted
robin perched on a small tree just outside the window. He vainly
thumped his beak at the glass. I was afraid he would break his
neck—or the window!

Next morning, right on cue, Mr. Robin was there, thumping
earnestly. I checked on him again and he seemed to peer in the glass.
I reluctantly lowered the shade so he couldn't see his reflection
and hurt himself. He returned to this spot for another two weeks.

Just as an eagle patrolled my home after Bill passed away, this
robin was paying me special attention. I've been told that a bird will
attack its reflection, mistaking the image for another bird invading

its territory. Was that the case? Perhaps. But I had never witnessed it before, and this bird seemed a special, feathered angel.

After Blair died, I bought a new computer and learned how to insert my photos properly into a slideshow. Working with the photos reminded me of the life I had with Blair and the wonderful things we did together. I wept as I scrolled through the images, choosing music—our music—to accompany the slides.

It hurt but it helped the healing. It was the same as a splinter is festering in your hand. You know something needs to be done, so you squeeze the festering wound and out comes the sliver. The pressure hurts. Later it feels better. In the same way, grief can produce the gut-wrenching pain of loss, the tears of sadness. But then you experience relief and sweet memories.

To work through my grief, I traveled. It had sounded like fun but it was hard to be alone. I didn't like seeing other couples holding hands in the airport terminals. I didn't like that I had no one to call to say I'd arrived—there wasn't anyone to wonder if I made it safely. Oh yes, my children cared, but they had their own lives. It wasn't the same as a husband, wondering if I made it safely to my destination. Yet traveling helped me process that I no longer had a mate. It was easier after navigating through the airport several times, finding a taxi, and staying in a hotel room alone. It was my life. A new life with myself.

Sunday afternoons were difficult. Worship was something I had shared with both of my spouses. But now, even though going to church was wonderful—hearing great preaching and singing songs that comforted me—after church, I was alone. I glanced at couples as they got into their cars together and wondered, *Do they know how fortunate they are to have each other?* I'd wish even more that I had appreciated it.

One Sunday afternoon, I sat in the great room, scrolling through my choices for a movie on television. Nothing looked good—another sure sign of grief: disinterest in watching or reading fiction. *Perhaps when there is intense drama in our lives, contrived drama seems meaningless.* The phone interrupted my thoughts and I picked it up to a familiar voice. It was Colleen.

"Would you like to go to a piano concert with me? Nathan wants to stay home and watch the Seahawks play so I thought of you!"

It took no longer than a heartbeat to say, "Yes. I'd love to go!"

So instead of being alone on a Sunday afternoon, I drove to the Newmark Theater, walked up its curvy stairs, and listened to one of my favorite instruments. We had perfect seats and sat back to enjoy Mozart, Beethoven, and then—my favorite—Chopin. The renowned pianist Richard Goode filled the hall with flashy and exuberant music. We were treated to two encores.

A Sunday surprise—another joy moment.

Life seemed to keep getting better. I was fortunate to live near some of my children and grandchildren. We went on hikes together. Celebrated birthdays together. Sometimes they would ask to spend the night at Grammie's and we'd watch movies and eat popcorn from my large king-sized bed.

It was good to be around friends and family. But there were times when that wasn't the case.

I'd had a date for coffee early that week and Peter told me he might give me a call. But he didn't—and I was disappointed.

Next morning, my daughter Erika called. "Hey Mom, want to hike up Angel's Rest with us today?"

"I don't know . . . I'm feeling kind of blue. You might not want me around," I said slowly.

"Oh, come on. You need the exercise. The kids want to see you."

I felt crummy. But she talked me into going and I pulled myself off my pity couch to grab my backpack.

We decided to meander down the Historic Columbia River Highway toward our destination. The late summer trees were beginning to lose their lustrous dark green for a faded, dusty emerald. Around every bend a beautiful waterfall filled the van windows with frothy splendor.

It was hazy in the midmorning light when we stopped to put on our hiking shoes—all except me. I discovered my hiking shoes were still at home and I was forced to wear my Teva sandals. *Great, now I'll get blisters!* I thought grumpily.

After the two-and-a-half mile hike up, we arrived to a 270-degree view of the beautiful gorge. The sun began to peek out of the clouds and I began to feel better. As we munched on our sandwiches, I pointed out Mount St. Helens, the city of Portland, and—faintly—our city of Vancouver.

Later that evening, I watched the movie *Tender Mercies*, starring Robert Duvall. I enjoyed the story of redemption but quietly ached for my own lover. I trudged up the stairs and went to bed.

Next morning, I woke with a sigh and felt that same emptiness inside, but I got out my Bible and read from Habakkuk 3:17-18.

Though the fig tree does not bud and there are no grapes on the vines, though the olive crop fails and fields produce no food, though there are no sheep in the pen and no cattle in the stalls, yet I will rejoice in the Lord, I will be joyful in God my Savior.

Okay, Lord, I prayed. *I will be joyful in You.* And I was.

I began to be grateful for the small joy moments in between the sad times of loss and grief. Those moments increased each day as I worked through the tough times. They only made me stronger.

CHAPTER 6

GRIEVING TAKES TIME— AND WORK

"There are no shortcuts to grieving. We're going through the pain in order to heal, because pain does heal."
—Dr. Susan Zonnebelt-Smeenge

Just as Dr. Smeenge stated, I found that I had to go through the pain to heal. I remembered the person I was grieving and reviewed his life. I allowed myself to address any regrets needing to be resolved. Even though my husband was dead and I couldn't talk to him, I could talk to God. I told Him those regrets and asked for forgiveness.

I wrote a letter to Blair, a goodbye of sorts, and put it aside. After a year, I visited his grave. I sat at his graveside in the warm sun and read aloud. "Oh my love, it tears my heart apart to say goodbye. I love you so much. My only regret is that we didn't have enough time."

After feeling those regrets, I learned to leave them in the past.

I did the work of grief by going through my loved one's personal items. I didn't rush the process of removing clothing from the closet. I waited for a while, comforted by the presence of my husband's clothes. The time came when they became a mocking reminder that the person was gone and I began to sort things. I gave some away and collected others in a memory box. A friend sewed a memory quilt for me with Bill's shirts. She lined the cozy throw with bright red flannel in a Tootsie Roll print. I could cuddle the fabric and remember him.

I did the work of grief through physical labor. I toiled away in the garage—not my usual place to clean and organize, but now there was no one else to do it and the process would encourage healing. I remembered Bill's garage, perfectly organized, everything in place: pegboards with tools and climbing equipment, hunting supplies, paint and wallpapering paraphernalia. It was a family joke that we could *eat* in the garage. This was Blair's garage, though—a little more cluttered and less organized.

Trent and Erika gave me a Christmas gift of cash to buy materials. Trent offered his time, building and assembling new shelves. I was excited to get started but surprised at each fresh wave of grief.

I came across garden gloves with the imprint of Blair's hand. I touched a floppy sun hat that kept freckles from accumulating on his face when he gardened. I felt the tears when moving his muddy gardening shoes or picking up the worn, wooden handle of his favorite rake.

I tossed duplicate prints of framed photos. I shredded old bank statements, classroom notes, and medical records. I separated garden tools, choosing the best and giving the rest away. I recycled half-used cans of paint and went to the garbage dump with accumulated junk. It felt good.

Trent put up rows of shelving, hung a hook for my bicycle, and assembled more stand-alone shelves. At last it was done. I wondered what either husband would have said had I been able to show them the finished product. Bill would have said, "Good job, gorgeous!" And Blair: "Well done, my sweetheart. You're a star!"

Moving forward had highs and lows. But I knew both husbands would be pleased that I continued to live my life.

One book instructed me to list my losses. It explained that some of those losses might have not been addressed. Just listing them, I was astounded at how many I'd experienced.

My preschool friend, Mary Lou, who drowned
My best friend Karen, killed in a car accident
A stillborn baby when I was thirty-one
The natural loss of my grandparents
My father

Bill, my first love and husband, who was only sixty-two years old
My second husband, Blair, after a mere seventeen months of marriage
My mother, only ten months after Blair died

I examined each of these deaths. I attended a group called GriefShare. Later, I led my own group as it continued to strengthen me in my loss and help me encourage others in theirs.

I learned that forgiveness is an important element of grief work. In my case, the person I grieved and needed to forgive was still living: Ron. Not only had he impulsively broken our engagement—he had also left me owing several thousand dollars. Originally, we had agreed that would he repay his half of the down payment and inspection fees when his retirement funds came in.

When I told him I thought he should pay his half, he said, "You have the finances. If the reverse had happened to me, I'd just pay for it myself." I thought his response was selfish, unmanly, and unchristian. I tried to regain the earnest money through small claims court but the contract was signed and the other party won the judgement.

As I worked through the disappointment, I realized that a marriage with Ron would have been difficult and tumultuous at best. Though there was money lost, it was not worth the trouble we would have had.

I needed to forgive Ron—no matter what. In my head, I knew I should. After all, the Lord's Prayer says to forgive, as we've been forgiven.

At first, I couldn't. I gave it time. Then I noticed upon waking up in the morning, *he* was not the first thing I thought about. I attended a women's retreat after the breakup. After a conversation, one listener said, "Sounds like you dodged a bullet." I hadn't thought of the breakup that way and realized she was right. I began to realize, whether he paid his part of the debt or not, I should forgive him.

We weren't right for each other. God answered my prayer—I was just surprised by how He did. I had received an answer I did not want but I needed to trust my future to the One who was in charge of it.

I needed to forgive—whether Ron paid back the money or not. After four months, Ron did pay his half of the debt, which gave me closure and healing.

We can experience other griefs in life, such as the grief of a failed marriage. Though my first marriage remained intact, I had many regrets regarding how we had handled the earlier years. We were fortunate to have worked out those dysfunctions. Sometimes that isn't possible. For a period of time, my sister Eileen, newly divorced, lived with me. She waited for the final decree and looked for a new place to live. She'd been married nearly forty years and tried so hard to make her marriage work. Even so, sometimes the best efforts don't change things. As we sipped our morning coffee, she looked at me with sad eyes and often asked, "Do you think I'm doing the right thing?"

We had many conversations about her marriage. She needed to repeat her story to an understanding person. She cried buckets of tears and I cried with her. But we laughed, too—just as in the past.

Losses include ill health, the grief of an empty nest, and the grief of time slipping away. Even a beautiful scene can bring a form of grief. I don't think anyone escapes grief during life. And that's how life is on this earth, as Solomon said in Ecclesiastes 3:1-4.

> There is a time for everything, and a season for every activity under heaven: a time to be born and a time to die, a time to plant and a time to uproot, a time to kill and a time to heal, a time to tear down and a time to build, a time to weep and a time to laugh, a time to mourn and a time to dance.

Grief and forgiveness are hard work. I was ready for some fun—and maybe a little dancing, too!

CHAPTER 7

JIM

"God came to us because God wanted to join us
on the road, to listen to our story, and to help
us realize that we are not walking in circles but
moving toward the house of peace and joy."
—Henri J. M. Nouwen

Living as a single person became my new normal. I had many
female friends. I traveled. Life was good. But there was still
something missing: a soulmate.

I tried several dating sites, going out with several men. One
man seemed like he a good prospect, but he was always busy
with his business. He wanted a companion—and a bed partner.
He'd been through a divorce and was leery of marrying again. "It's
complicated," he said when I asked about his situation.

I told him that I believed sex before marriage was wrong. I
wanted someone like Bill or Blair—someone who was crazy about
me and wanted to be with *me*. And just like Bill and Blair, they
needed to agree with my belief that only sex after marriage was the
right choice. Of course, I wanted other qualities as well—such as
a love for God and a desire to serve Him. This man needed to love
his own family as well as mine and see eye-to-eye with my political
views. Was there someone like that out there?

After Ron, I was determined not to connect with the wrong
person again. I joined a new dating site, taking a long personality
quiz about what I wanted for my future.

I invited my sister Eileen and two friends, Judi and Jane, for
girl talk and a game of dominoes. All single, we sat at my table
discussing the usual—guys, dating, and marriage.

"I need to meet someone soon," Jane said, "or it will be too late. I'll be too old—and so will he. I'd rather be alone than take care of someone in poor health. After all, I had a good marriage. Maybe I'll just live on good memories!"

"I'm too old and set in my ways to meet someone," Judi put in. "I think I'll stay single. After all, John has been gone twelve years now."

I finished writing down our scores and laid the pencil down. "I hear you both. But I'm not ready to give up on a marriage partner just yet. I think the right guy is out there, waiting."

Next morning, Judi invited me to her home for a Labor Day barbecue and I busily put together a pasta salad. I sat down in my morning room to read my Bible and devotional, *Streams in the Desert*.⁵ I reflected on our conversation the night before and wondered about a new matching service. *If this doesn't work, Lord, I won't do any more searching*, I prayed. My future match would not come about by my manipulating someone into being the right person. *You will just have to drop him in my lap! And Lord,* I thought with a smile. *Would you make him crazy about me—and love You more than I do?* I felt settled when I left it up to Him.

There was still a hole in my life that I wanted filled. I truly tried to fill it with other interests.

The new dating service sent me photos of men with their profiles. Some I'd met on other sites. To my chagrin, some I'd already dated!

Then, a bright Sunday morning, a new guy came in to view. Five-foot-ten. He sounded like a widower, though I wasn't positive. He lived across the river in the Columbia River Gorge and was cute, too. It was *what* he said, though, that really got my attention. Jim was a strong, committed Christian who was obviously not ashamed of his faith. He loved his family, too.

The matching service asked, "What makes a relationship?" and Jim had answered:

1. Honesty
2. Financial security
3. Affection in touch and words
4. Love of family and acceptance of partner's family

Even these answers were similar to mine. *Hmmm . . . !*

After several question exchanges, he sent me a message. "Would you like to meet for coffee?"

"Sure," I responded. "But let's keep emailing." We exchanged our personal email addresses and continued to reveal more of ourselves to each other. He told me his last name and I Googled him, confirming that the resume he sent me was very similar. This guy was thorough! There didn't seem to be any secrets.

Later that week, I attended a Women's Connection Brunch and set my silenced cell phone on the table. While listening to a presentation, I noticed a phone call with an area code from the Portland area. *Could it be Jim?* I quickly went outside to listen to the voicemail. Sure enough, I heard an enthusiastic voice saying, "Wow, this feels kind of strange, but I'm wondering if you'd like to meet for coffee this morning? Give me a call and let's see if we can set a date!" I felt a surge of electricity as I immediately called back and we agreed on twelve thirty that afternoon. We were to meet at a nearby Starbucks just across the river. I smiled in excitement. What might this meeting be like?

I was a bit late as I drove into the crowded parking lot. Meeting someone for the first time is always an adventure. I braced myself for the disappointment I'd experienced so many times. But then I found myself thinking optimistically, imagining that things would be different this time. The sun peeked through the clouds as I stepped past outdoor tables scattered with people. I glanced inside. Nearby stood a trim man dressed in jeans and polo shirt with a full head of salt-and-pepper hair. His back was to me as he surveyed the crowded lunchtime group.

"Are you Jim?"

He turned to me, friendly blue eyes framed by wire, square glasses. He flipped his laptop open, looked at my profile photo on the screen and said, "You must be Shirley." We shook hands and Jim asked what he could get for me.

"A cappuccino, please. A tall would be great." He came back with our drinks and we began to talk nonstop.

Jim was indeed a widower as I suspected. When two people meet who share a similar loss—in our case, a spouse—there is an understanding. Unlike relationships ended through other ways, there is no threat when speaking of a late spouse. There are only sweet memories. Jim asked about my losses and I told him about Bill's leukemia and death. I went on to relate how I met and married Blair two years later. On our last evening together, Blair lost consciousness due to a brain aneurysm and died. Jim shook his head in sympathy. "What about you?" I asked.

"My wife Kathy had been tired for several months," he explained. "At first we blamed it on getting older, but we started wondering when she got so short of breath that she needed my help pushing her garden cart. We found out she had pulmonary fibrosis in 2008."

I stumbled over the unfamiliar term and Jim replied, "Well, it was actually idiopathic pulmonary fibrosis—IPF. It causes a person to slowly suffocate." Jim shook his head at the memory of her struggling for air during her last days. "Some people get a lung transplant but Kathy didn't want to be tied to the medical system for the rest of her life."

"Wow, you've been through a lot."

"Well, no more than you," he countered. "I sold my business to take care of her. Even though those were the hardest years, they were also the best. We were forced to slow down. We talked through our difficult years and forgave each other for the mistakes we had made. This battle of her disease was our battle together."

This guy is quality, I thought.

"I really loved Psalm 119 and read it over and over to her. God was good, for she died peacefully. One late summer day at 4:20 in the afternoon, her breathing slowed and quietly—painlessly—she slipped into eternity. My Kathy was gone." His voice broke.

I brushed away tears. *Such a profound event of life.* "Was Kathy the first person you saw die?"

"No, I've been with a lot of family members in their last moments, beginning with my father, when I was thirty years old. It is an honor to be with someone when they make the passage from this earth to the next life." Jim sipped his coffee and continued his story. "Two days after Kathy died, I was outside working in my yard. My neighbor Sarah asked if Kathy died. When I confirmed, she told me a story.

"I was out on my lawn tractor, mowing the upper field next to your place," Sarah began. "It was noisy, but beyond the mower sound, I heard bells ringing. You know, like church bells clanging together in celebration." She paused. "I heard people cheering like at a sporting event. I heard this over the sound of my mower. It was *loud*. Now that you've told me the time, it makes sense. I think heaven was celebrating Kathy's entry. It was 4:20."

"Amazing," I said.

Jim nodded and went on. "I've had my share of losses. In 2007, my daughter Kara died in her sleep and her husband, Aaron, found her. They determined it was sleep apnea. His father was so traumatized, we cared for our grandson, Cole, for more than a year and became very close to him."

"What's the name of your book?" Jim asked, changing the subject. *This guy wants to get to know me,* I thought gleefully.

We clicked. It seemed as though we could keep on talking forever. Jim chuckled at one point and said, "I think there's some chemistry going on here!" I smiled at his quip, glad he felt that way—but held back a little, not wanting to reveal too much too soon.

"I'd like to say a prayer about our relationship. Would you mind?" he put in.

Would I mind? I thought. My heart soared. We bowed our heads in the busy coffee shop, oblivious to others around us. "Oh Heavenly Father," Jim prayed. "Be with us as we explore our relationship. Would you show us what we need to see? I ask this in Jesus' name." He paused for a moment. "And all God's people said," he stopped again. "Amen!" we said in unison. We smiled at each other, both hoping this might be something good and right.

"I'd like to go to worship service with you at your church this Sunday. What do you think?"

I hesitated for a moment. "Well, I won't be going to my own church this Sunday. The church my father pastored for twelve years is celebrating their one hundred and fiftieth anniversary."

"It doesn't matter which church we go to—I'd just like to go with you!" he responded. "How about I pick you up? We could have coffee and you could show me your house."

"That sounds good."

"It's a *date*, then!" Jim put his hands out with enthusiasm.

Our coffee cups long drained, we got up to leave. Jim walked me into the parking lot. "I like your car. It says something about you. And you like red!"

"I do." We said goodbye and Jim gave me a sideways hug. He pulled away, slowly, as though he didn't want to let go. I didn't want him to, either.

Wow. That was good, I thought as I drove away, late for my next appointment.

Jim went to visit old friends in eastern Oregon and while he was gone, we sent playful and friendly texts. We exchanged emails with even more detail about our families. Each of us wrote out our family trees.

Jim grew up in Portland in a large Catholic family of eight children, all quite close.

Saturday night, the phone rang. It was Jim. "Shirley. I just finished reading your book. I began after I got home from Tygh Valley and did not get out of my chair until I turned the last page. I am so moved by your story. If it weren't so late, I'd ask if I could come over and just give you a hug." We talked for a while longer and he said again, "The words from your book just blew me away." He paused. "I wish I could be with you."

I chimed in, "You're welcome to come over if you want to make the drive!"

"Great! I'll be there in less than an hour. See you soon."

I quickly got out of my pajamas, put on shorts and T-shirt and waited in the warm night for him to come. As I saw his headlights turn into my driveway, I walked out to greet him.

He burst out of the car, reaching for me with a hard yet friendly hug. "Thank you so much for your book. I enjoyed it very much. I felt like I was right there with you."

"Thank you." I felt awkward. My book revealed so much about myself and my soul that Jim knew more about me than I knew about him. I felt a loss for words so I just reached out and hugged Jim again. He responded with another strong squeeze. We slowly parted, smiled at each other, and walked in the growing darkness of the warm evening up my steep driveway. Inside, we shared a glass of wine and talked for several hours. It was as if we'd known each other for years, not days. There were no empty silences or awkward moments, only a sweet sense of being comfortable.

We hugged one last time and I watched the taillights of his car disappear down the street. I sighed with contentment.

Next morning, we had our coffee as planned and I showed Jim around the house, pointing out photos of family members. He remembered names from my book. The church music was stirring with a cacophony of drums playing the introduction and the choir joining in. Each time a leader would pray, Jim would take my hand, releasing it at the end of the prayer.

The worship leader instructed, "Greet the people sitting near you. Meet old friends." Eileen stepped down from the choir to greet us. Jim gave her a hug and said, "Do you know what a wonderful sister you have?"

She chuckled. "Yes!" Later she told me she had observed us from her perch in the choir. She could see Jim worshiping with pleasure and she thought his smile was extra wide because I was seated next to him.

After the worship service, I stood with Jim in the picnic buffet line, joined by my daughter Erika and her family. Jim and my son-in-law Trent chatted about being an entrepreneur in the home repair business. Jim found a seat in the hot sun and joked easily with my four grandchildren. He asked the girls if they liked VeggieTales and learned about their Awana group. "I used to be the commander at my church!" he exclaimed.

"Who's your favorite football team?" Jim asked the boys.

"My favorite team is the Seahawks," said Andrew. "Caleb likes the Broncos."

"Well, Andrew, we like the same football team," said Jim. "I sure hope they make it to Super Bowl this year!"

After the picnic, we drove to Jim's home near Springdale in the Sandy River Gorge. He owned a renovated farmhouse originally built in the 1920s. The three-acre parcel of land was beautifully landscaped. Jim's late wife was a master gardener and together they had created a quiet, woodsy haven that reminded me of California's Napa Valley. We relaxed in deck chairs, looking out over a hillside nursery in the distance. "Oh, it's beautiful!" I exclaimed.

"It is," he agreed, "but it was Kathy's project more than mine. It requires a lot of work that I'm no longer excited to do."

"Would you be willing to go on a weekend trip to the Ashland Shakespeare Festival?" he asked suddenly. "We could get tickets for a couple of plays and really get to know each other while we are on the five-hour drive. Of course we'd get separate rooms." He offered a shy smile, wanting me to feel safe.

"I think I'd like that."

Jim logged on to order tickets for *My Fair Lady* and *Cymbeline*. This would be fun!

In the kitchen, Jim turned on the happy sounds of the Hawaiian version of "Over the Rainbow." I tapped my feet to the beat and then "Unchained Melody" came on. Jim extended his hand and asked, "Shall we dance?" I took his hand and put my arm on his shoulder as he put his hand on my back and we slowly swayed to the music.

Our conversation never stopped as we drove to nearby Columbia River Gorge and climbed a trail near Multnomah Falls. On our way back, we stopped for dinner at Tad's Chicken and Dumplings. As we waited for our table, we sat outside on the deck and looked out on the Sandy River in the late summer evening. The pre-autumn air was balmy as we watched the sun disappear and the darkening sky take its place.

"Tell me about your family," he said. "I *really* want to get to know you."

"Well, I need to start at the beginning, before I was born . . . "

CHAPTER 8

HENRY AND ROSE

"A heritage is the spiritual, emotional, and social legacy
that is passed from parent to child . . . good or bad."[6]
—J. Otis Ledbetter & Kurt Bruner

Paul Meyer was born at the Salvation Army Rescue Hospital in Omaha, Nebraska. His sixteen-year-old mother, Adelia Lloyd, was not married. Who was the father? There is speculation he was her employer and she a maid in the household. His last name was Meyer and he was listed as thirty-six years old. Did Meyer take advantage of her station? Was it simply lust—or did they share love? Did Adelia marry one day? Did Paul have other brothers and sisters? Did Adelia's heart nearly break as she signed the adoption papers and said goodbye to her baby at the orphanage?

So it was that my father came into the world, cared for at the Salvation Army Orphanage until he was six months old. Questions remain which my family will never be able to answer, as the records at the Hamilton County Courthouse were burned in 2002.

In a small farming community west of Omaha, a childless couple, Anna and Cornelius P. Quiring very much wanted a child. Anna wanted a girl. Cornelius—or CP as he was called—wanted a boy. They were both of German descent—"Hollanders." Their parents had emigrated from Holland to Germany and then on to what is now Ukraine. The laws were changing and included forced conscription. For the Hollanders, who were Mennonites, this was unacceptable. Family by family, they immigrated to the United

States and homesteaded in Nebraska. In their very close community, most of the Hollanders spoke German in their homes and churches.

On March 7, 1918, the agency told them there was a baby boy available for adoption and they drove more than one hundred miles to pick him up. As soon as the undersized infant was placed in her arms, Anna fell in love, no longer caring whether she held son or daughter. They named him Henry.

Anna and CP were both Christians and attended one of the numerous Mennonite congregations near their home in Henderson, Nebraska. Their farm was large and profitable, the land rich, and CP was an excellent farmer. In contrast to the poverty of city families during the Great Depression, Henry didn't lack for much. As Henry grew, he was sometimes lonesome, vowing that when he was married, there'd be more than one child in his family.

Henry was easygoing and enjoyed people. Handsome, broad-chested, and fairly tall at five ten, with curly blonde hair and blue eyes, he was strong and a hard worker. When he was sixteen, Henry accepted Christ as his personal Savior with a strong desire to serve and follow Him. He believed God was calling him to be a missionary to Africa.

One September day, a new family moved into town. What interested Henry was the blonde, blue-eyed seventeen-year-old girl named Rose.

Rose was born in Zurich, Montana, a tiny community in the eastern part of the state, close to the Canadian border—a town that doesn't exist anymore. Her parents' names were Sara and Jacob, known as Jake. Both of their families were Mennonite Hollanders.

The family moved several times, trying to find good crop-producing land. On one farm, locusts destroyed the crops and the following year, a root-eating worm eradicated the wheat crop. And then, the terrible dust storms that devastated the Midwest and Oklahoma invaded their land. To keep the house clean, Sara put damp cloths on the screens to prevent the dust from coming into the house. When the wind died down, the cloths were black with dust.

Through it all, Sara was the rock for her family, especially young Rose. Her mother was the person she shared her joys and sorrows with. Sara was a vibrant Christian, gently guiding Rose to a stronger faith in God.

In 1933, Rose's parents were forced to auction off their farm. The crop failure, caused by locust infestation, left them unable to meet their payments at the bank. Jake heard they were hiring laborers at the new dam at Fort Peck on the Missouri River.

The family found a house to rent in the new community—a humble, roughly-built cabin—and went to work making it inviting.

It was a cold, late Saturday afternoon in January when Jake brought home a roll of linoleum after his shift at the dam. He nailed the floor while Sara placed a rag rug in front of the davenport. Then father and son moved the black cast-iron range into place, connecting the stove pipe to the back of the stove and up into the ceiling. With the new range, Sara could once again make her famous crusty bread and zwiebacks: those flaky, buttery dinner rolls the Mennonites are known for. In a few minutes, Sara had the fire crackling and their supper steaming.

The younger sisters, Margaret and Ruth, sat on one side of the table. Rose, the eldest at seventeen, sat beside her brother Arnold. Jake was at the head of the table and Sara at the foot. The room was warm and fragrant with beef borscht and cabbage soup. "Phew! I'm tired!" Sara declared. "Jake, ask the blessing."

"This soup is wery good, Sara," Jake announced in his German accent as he spread chokecherry jam on his roll. "May I have seconds?" He held up his bowl. "Vhat's this?" he asked, spying the stemmed goblets that held dessert. "Wanilla pudding? You know it's my favorite!"

"Mmm," Ruth declared, reaching for her pudding.

"Not yet, girlie, you need to clean your bowl first!" Jake said sternly.

"I've got another headache," Sara said, rubbing her temples and forehead. She pushed aside her full bowl. "I suppose it's from all the work on that floor tonight."

"It's your high blood pressure," said Jake. "Why don't you lie down, Sara. Rosie and the girls will clean up the dishes."

"Can I have Mama's pudding?" Ruth asked.

"No, I want it!" Margaret chimed in.

"Certainly not, girls! That's your mama's and she will eat it later!" Rose scolded.

Sara lay sideways on the davenport while Jake adjusted her legs to make her more comfortable.

"Should I call the doctor?" Jake asked Sara, pausing to take a long look at her pale face.

"No, don't bother. I'll be better after I rest awhile."

Her breathing became labored as she lay, eyes closed.

"Dad," Rose exclaimed after a minute had passed. "I think you should get the doctor. Mama looks very sick!"

Moments later, the doctor bustled in, opened his bag, and placed the stethoscope on Sara's chest. He listened carefully, then opened her closed eyelids, and flashed the ophthalmoscope into her eyes. He shook his head and turned to Jake. "I'm sorry, this doesn't look good. I think she's suffered a brain aneurysm."

"Vhat's that you said?" Jake said. "An aneurysm? Is that serious?"

"I think a blood vessel has ruptured."

"Can we do something?" Jake covered his face as he wept.

"I'm sorry. There's nothing we can do; the broken blood vessel has poisoned the brain tissue."

After several minutes, Sara labored one last sigh. The room was silent. The doctor placed the stethoscope on Sara's chest one last time. "I'm sorry. She's gone."

"Oh, Sara! No!" Jake covered his face as he wept.

"Mama!" Margaret and Ruth wailed. Rose came over to the bed, knelt beside her mother and took her hand. "She can't be gone," Rose sobbed. "Oh, Mama, come back. I don't want you to go!"

Sara Schroeder Richert, age forty-two, was now in heaven and the family would never be the same.

Jake made the necessary arrangements for the funeral. Sara was to be buried in Lustre, Montana, about sixty miles from their home in Fort Peck. It was an all-day trip to the church and cemetery for the burial. There had been heavy snowstorms and the roads weren't graded or plowed. During the treacherous journey, Sara's coffin fell out of the truck into the snowy road twice before they arrived at the funeral home, filling the children with a sense of grief, loss, and panic all over again. None of the family were ready to say goodbye; Sara was far too young.

Rose was now in charge of the home. Rose took over the cooking, cleaning, and sewing. She was a capable young woman but still an inexperienced teenager. Jake complained about her cooking, saying, "Ah, this fish isn't as good as your mother used to make." He would get up from the table and pace back and forth in the small house, crying silently.

Rose took in laundry, allowing herself only one small pleasure: a weekly visit to the beauty parlor to have her hair crimped into Marcel waves.

Rose missed her mother profoundly. There were times when Rose wanted to talk about her mother but people would change the subject, thinking it hurt too much. Little did they know, it was exactly what would help her grief.

After a few months, Jake began corresponding with a woman in Henderson, Nebraska: a widow with four children. Without ever setting eyes on each other, Jake asked Lena to marry him, and within six months, the family moved to Henderson, blending to become a family of ten. It was a marriage of necessity. Lena was a gruff, stout German woman who didn't tolerate challenges to her authority. She seemed harder on the girls, expecting them to pull their weight in the household duties. Soon there were squabbles and arguments between Jake and Lena. The honeymoon was over—if there ever had been one.

Jake and the children missed Sara terribly. Sara's death affected Rose for the remainder of her life. Countless times while working together doing household chores, Mom would retell the story of her mother's sudden death. The retelling prepared me for what was to come in my own life.

Times were tough in the mid-1930s and the family struggled to keep food on the table. The older teenage boys worked at part-time jobs while attending school. Rose helped in Anna Quiring's kitchen, cooking meals, washing clothes, and cleaning house.

It was here, working for his mother, that Rose caught Henry's eye. As their courtship began, they studied the Bible and prayed together. One evening as they sat in his car, Henry asked Rose, "To what do you think God is calling you?"

"To be a missionary nurse," she answered. "In the Belgian Congo."

"That's where I think God wants me to serve as a missionary, too!" Henry burst out.

On Rose's twentieth birthday, October 3, 1937, they were married.

Henry and Rose on their wedding day, October 3, 1937

Henry and Rose lived in the farmhouse with his parents for a few years. They had their first child, Joyce. They were busy working the farm and serving their church, but Henry was miserable. He reasoned that he could be a wealthy farmer and contribute money to the mission field rather than go himself. Yet it wasn't enough. Though he was set to inherit a fertile and well-established farm, he still felt the persistent call from God.

Finally, they left their home in Nebraska and enrolled at Moody Bible Institute in Chicago, intending to obtain degrees and go to a foreign mission field. Their son Roger was born while they both worked and attended school, raising their two young children.

My parents' full-time ministry unfolded—not on a foreign field but on American soil with my father as a pastor and my mother as his full-time helpmate in the ministry.

Henry was friendly and outgoing—a "man's man", as my mother would say. His farming roots showed in his strength and stamina. His churches were fairly small but grew under his leadership. His sermons were down-to-earth, filled with stories from his youth and simple, daily living. He stayed true to Scripture, choosing a book of the Bible to preach from in exposition style, rather than topical.

Mom taught, counseled, and infused artistry into their work. She used charcoal, oil paint, and chalk to transfix children and adults as she taught lessons, earning awards throughout her life.

"I wish I could have met your parents. When do you come into the picture?" Jim asked me.

"Hang on, I'm almost there!" I joked as I relayed my stories.

"I'm all ears! I want to know everything!"

CHAPTER 9

HERE I COME!

"What's past is prologue."
—William Shakespeare, *The Tempest*

World War II had been over for a year. Mom and Dad were attending Bible school and summer break was approaching. They drove home from Chicago to Nebraska, using their hard-earned savings to treat the family to a hotel stay in Omaha. The little family had supper in a nearby restaurant and settled into bed for the night.

"Mama, I don't feel good," Joyce complained.

"I don't feel so good either," Roger moaned.

Rose felt their foreheads and tucked the covers around them. "I'm not feeling well, either," she whispered to Henry, holding her very pregnant stomach.

"What do you think we should do?"

Rose shook her head. "I can't tell whether or not these are labor pains. But I don't want to have this baby in Omaha!"

In the middle of the night, Rose and Henry packed their belongings and set out for the small town of York, one hundred miles away, with no Interstate. During the all-night drive, they stopped frequently along the road because the children were so sick. In the evening of the next day, May 6, I came into the world.

My parents planned to find an apartment while they both continued at Moody Bible Institute. Dad would continue his part-time work at a warehouse. But something happened in Chicago that changed their plans.

With war veterans seeking homes, housing was scarce. Dad found two apartments on separate floors of a building: one with a living room and bedroom, another with a kitchen and second bedroom. He decided both apartments together could meet their needs and signed the papers, ready to get back to work and bring his family to their new home.

Henry walked into the busy personnel office at Montgomery Ward in Chicago. The clerk glanced up at the young man standing in front of her desk, holding his cap in his hands. "May I help you?"

"I'm here to fill out the paperwork," Henry said. "Joe Witczak told me he'd hold my job open until August."

The clerk sorted through a card file and looked at Henry. "I'm sorry, that warehouse job has been filled. They needed someone right away."

Henry felt his throat go dry and cleared his throat nervously. "Isn't there something? I really needed that job. My family's coming into town next week."

"I'm sorry. There just isn't anything." She turned away and began typing briskly. Henry walked away slowly, shaking his head. *What am I going to do?*

Now they had a very inconvenient dwelling for a family of five with a newborn and no job. After a week of looking for work—living on bologna sandwiches, instant coffee, and a bag of apples—Henry cried out, "Oh God, what should I do?"

Dad realized it was an impossible situation and gave notice to the landlord that the family would not be living there after all. He drove the two days' journey back home to Henderson.

"Daddy's home!" Joyce and Roger cried excitedly, as Henry entered the driveway of the Grace Children's Home. The family had been living temporarily in a guest cottage. It was—and still is—a home for troubled youth, founded by a local pastor to provide a safe, Christian atmosphere.

Henry got out of the car and gave the children a hug, looking up at Rose with concern. "We're going to have to think of something else to do." He went on to tell her of the job and apartment situation.

"We just have to trust God to take care of us and show us what to do," she said.

Henry made enquiries. Evangelical Mennonite Brethren Church, Henry's home church, was without a pastor. One day there was a voice on the phone, a member of the the pastoral search committee calling Henry. "Would you consider coming to our church?" Henry and Rose prayed and decided this was where God was calling them. Instead of finishing their education, they accepted the call and settled into a large home with bedrooms for everyone, a vegetable garden, and a new sense of security.

And so I lived with my family in Nebraska until I was four, when something would happen that would transform my life.

CHAPTER 10

LIFE-CHANGING EVENT

"Jesus loves me! He who died
Heaven's gate to open wide;
He will wash away my sin,
Let His little child come in."
—Anna B. Warner

My dad was tending the church cemetery grounds while Roger and I played nearby. We wandered through the bumpy hillocks of the grassy cemetery, looking at markers. "Henry Wiens. Born September 9, 1885. Died July 10, 1916. He must have died in the War," my brother read. "Here's another one: Nellie Harms. Born May 1, 1855. Died December 12, 1945." We meandered through the cemetery as Roger continued to read the names. I could see my daddy on the far side of the cemetery, briskly pushing the mower.

"Where is Mary Lou's grave?" I asked. My special friend from Sunday School had fallen into the rain-swollen creek and drowned. The tragic accident had been the talk of our small farming community.

"Here." He pointed out a newly planted headstone. The grass was not yet grown over the raw, small plot. He read, "Mary Lou Goertzen. Born January 12, 1946. Died May 29, 1950."

"Where is she now?"

"Her body's down there, in the ground," he said. I shivered at the thought. Roger continued, "But her soul—the part that thinks for you—is in heaven. With Jesus."

"I want to go to heaven when I die," I said, swallowing through my thickening throat. The idea of being anywhere else—far from God and family—terrified me.

"All you have to do is pray. Just ask Jesus. He'll come in."

I remembered a children's song I'd sung in Sunday School with Mary Lou.

> Into my heart, into my heart,
> Come into my heart, Lord Jesus;
> Come in today, come in to stay;
> Come into my heart, Lord Jesus.[7]

Roger was nearly eight years old. Handsome, with curly blonde hair and bright blue eyes, he enthusiastically told his friends about Jesus. In simple trust, I believed my brother's message of faith. I knelt by Mary Lou's grave and said something like this: "Dear Jesus. I want to be in heaven with You when I die. I'm sorry for the things I've done wrong."

"Like having a temper tantrum?" Roger offered. My brother and I were rivals most of our growing years, and he teased me unmercifully. Now, even though I was his newest convert, he couldn't resist the chance to remind me of my faults. "What about lying when Mama asked if you hit me?"

"Yes, Jesus," I continued, my eyes closed and hands folded. "I'm sorry. I want to be with You. Please come into my heart. Help me be good."

I meant every word of that simple prayer. It was just as real and heartfelt as if I'd prayed at twice that age. That decision was permanent and life-changing. My life certainly wasn't perfect and problem-free because of that decision. But I do know I was protected from many potentially bad choices because of my faith in Jesus and the presence of the Holy Spirit.

Later that afternoon, Roger and I walked into the house where Mama was busily making supper for the family of six. She was holding Eileen in her arms while frying chicken in the pan and stirring gravy for our meat and potatoes. "Mama, Mama!" I shouted. "I asked Jesus into my heart."

"You did?" Mama put down the fork and knelt down to my level. She gave me a hug and asked, "Do you know what that means?"

"Yes. It means I'm going to heaven to be with Jesus—and with all of you!" I said, almost at the top of my voice. "Roger told me all I needed to do was ask for Jesus to come in. He did—I know he did!"

Dad was going through his own life-changing event at this time. He realized he needed to finish his education. His doctrinal beliefs were changing and both my parents felt it was time to leave the Mennonites.

In late summer 1950, our family of six packed up our belongings, purchased a small trailer, and moved to Portland where Dad would attend Western Conservative Baptist Seminary. Our Grandpa and Grandma Richert lived in nearby Dallas and we stayed with them for a few days while Mom and Dad looked for a place to live.

It was difficult. Housing was scarce once again, this time because of the Korean War. It took several weeks to find a rental home. The family would pack up each morning and drive the eighty-some miles to Portland where our parents would pore over both newspapers, looking at the classifieds for housing. For extra cash, they went to the fields to pick hops. Finally, they found a one-bedroom. We packed into this small house, yet it never felt crowded. The important thing was that we were together.

One morning, while Dad was waiting in the seminary admissions office, a woman walked into the room. "Do you have a list of preachers who could come to our church? We need someone starting next Sunday," she said breathlessly.

"I'm a pastor," Henry said firmly, standing. He brushed his blonde hair back on his nearly bald head, smiled, and met her eye with confidence. My dad knew he needed to take care of his family and this was an opportunity for him. He was confident he could do the job. It wasn't the first or last time he reached out for opportunities to provide for his family. Later, when we lived in the country, he supplemented our family income by working part-time during the growing season in a nearby cannery. Any time an opportunity for a job with higher wages was posted, he'd apply for it. He wasn't afraid to try something new. "I can do that," he'd say. Evidently the employers believed him, for he usually got the job.

"What's your experience?" the woman asked.

"I left my former church two months ago. I was there for four years but now I'm attending seminary to finish my education."

"Can you give me some references?"

Apparently the search committee liked his references, for they called Dad to be the interim pastor at University Park Congregational Church in north Portland. Dad would receive a small stipend and our family would have better housing. Our new home, "the brown house", sat on Oberlin Street.

I loved that house. A full basement stored sawdust that fueled the furnace. There was a big square grate in the dining room that heated the lower story of the house. On cold mornings, I'd hurry downstairs to dress over the grate, where the updraft from the furnace blew my skirt out and warmed my legs.

Mom taught us to memorize what has become my favorite scripture: Psalm 23. I'd recite it as I skipped through the house. Sometimes, I'd stand over the grate while I practiced. "The Lord is my shepherd, I shall not want . . ."

We moved one more time to southeast Portland when my parents purchased a home—a small, unfinished two-bedroom. Huge fir trees and overgrown brush abounded in that lot. Little did I know that the brush was poison oak; soon I was covered with the itchy rash. Mom used a smelly brown ointment to help the nearly intolerable itching.

I'll never forget first grade. Because of that poison oak, I had to start school two weeks late. Roger walked me to school and introduced me to my teacher. As we entered the classroom, we heard the hum of children's voices settling down for their day of learning. I was excited but nervous. At last, I'd be able to read! I loved hearing stories and even pretended I could read to my little sister, Eileen. My young teacher, Miss Haug, was probably in the first year of her job. She greeted me with a frown instead of a welcoming smile.

As I look back at the classroom photograph, I understand. She was overburdened with thirty-four little first graders in that room and here was one more student to catch up by two weeks. Though I was frightened by her scowl, she was simply overwhelmed!

I showed her my supplies. There was a Big Chief writing tablet, bright red with a black headdress of an Indian chief on the front, and two bright orange pencils with white lines on the ridges. I was so proud of them.

"You won't be able to use those pencils," Miss Haug said, her voice rising with impatience. "You'll need to get a primary pencil."

I was crushed. I loved those orange pencils! I took one and broke it in half.

"Why did you do that?" she scolded.

"I don't know," I said tearfully. Deep down, I did know why: I was angry. I didn't get to do what *I* wanted to.

"Well, never mind. Here," she said impatiently, "you can sit next to Bonnie." I placed my things on the desk next to a dark-haired, brown-eyed girl who looked up at me from her seat with a smile. At last, I was in first grade. I'd learn how to read and write. And someday, I'd get to use that orange pencil!

It's a family joke that I have the most advanced degree of the five of us. I'm the only sibling who attended kindergarten. And though it would be years before I learned to tame my stubborn streak, I did learn to write with a bright orange pencil that year.

CHAPTER 11

QUESTIONS

"The most important questions in life can never
be answered by anyone except oneself."
—John Fowles

Jim and I were sitting side by side on the couch in my living room. He held my hand as he listened to the stories of my life. He cleared his throat and asked, "Didn't you tell me you were engaged not long ago?"

"Yes," I said. I looked down, ashamed, fingering the afghan on the couch. "I wasn't over Blair yet and I just felt a little bit crazy because I didn't want to be alone. It's the only way I can explain myself."

Jim looked at me thoughtfully as I told him the story of the aborted engagement. "I understand perfectly. I was engaged too," he said, shaking his head. "I'm pretty sure I asked her to marry me because I was so lonely and just wanted the pain of Kathy's death behind me. I wanted to forget. It was hard."

I asked to hear more, surprised by our similar stories.

"Even though we had faith in common, it really wasn't enough. She had an abusive past and I don't think she healed from those abuses." He stopped for a moment. "I think I was trying to save her—you know, the knight in shining armor who saves the damsel in distress."

I wondered quietly to myself. *Will he try to save me? Is he really over Kathy?*

Little did I know, Jim was having thoughts of his own. *Are we moving too fast? Can I ever match up to the two husbands Shirley's had? Has she really finished grieving Blair? Is she still stuck on Ron?*

I really liked this guy and wanted to believe he was who he said he was. Only time would tell.

"Let's talk about something else," Jim said, changing the subject. "Did you stay and finish school in Portland?"

I continued the story that was special to me, hoping he'd think so, too.

CHAPTER 12

THE MID YEARS

"It is the sweet, simple things of life
which are the real ones after all."
—Laura Ingalls Wilder

Haley Baptist Church was located in the foothills of Oregon's tallest peak, Mount Hood. Hills, berry fields, and nurseries dotted the landscape. On one side of our house was a strawberry patch. Across the street was a family-owned nursery filled with cultivated Japanese iris. Behind the house was a big field of tall grasses where we enjoyed playing in late summer.

The parsonage was next door to the church. It was a "shotgun house"—a straight shot from back to front. It could never be compared to the home of a middle-class family today, as there was just one bathroom—a tub, no shower—for seven people, shared bedrooms for siblings, and a back porch converted into a bedroom for the only boy in the family.

Eileen and I were—and still are—best buds. Only twenty-two months apart, we were often asked if we were twins. Called "the girls" from toddlerhood, we were two blue-eyed towheads in crisp, dotted swiss pastel dresses. We looked like angels but played hard, fought like cats and dogs, and loved fiercely. We were well-dressed in spite of Dad's low salary, because our mom was an excellent seamstress. She prowled J.C. Penney or Newberry's in downtown Portland for fabric bargains.

Saturday night was bath night. It was convenient for us to bathe and wash our hair together. Mom would put curlers in my hair but

Eileen's naturally curly hair didn't need them. In the morning, my nearly white-blonde hair would be full of curls.

Dressing up on Sunday was expected and I felt special walking across the driveway to climb the stairs to the church in my Sunday attire. I was a shy girl, glad to have my younger sister with me. I felt that together, we could do anything.

Eileen and I shared a bedroom—and a bed—nearly all of our growing years. We devised ways to separate our sides, with a dramatic difference between the two. She was the messy and I was the clean-y. That has changed since for I've relaxed and Eileen has become much more particular about keeping her home neat with everything in place.

The two of us would snuggle in the double bed and whisper plans for play the next day. What would we do? Go to the woods and have a picnic? How about playing house in our friend Darlene's empty chicken coop?

That strawberry patch next door tempted us to pick and taste. The field did not belong to us, though, and we didn't have permission to take any of the juicy red orbs. One morning, Mama glanced out the kitchen window and noticed we were sampling those berries. Dad sat us down and talked about how we don't take from others—not even one bite. He reminded us that even picking a flower from a neighbor's yard was stealing. Both of us were spanked for that deed, and even now, I cannot sample one grape from the produce section in the grocery store unless it is offered to me, so strong was that early lesson.

Eileen and I shared friends. Darlene, and occasionally her brother Ernie, roamed the woods with us and put on plays for our families. Once, the two younger girls coaxed me to jump from the roof into the tall grass. "The grass is soft; you won't hurt yourself," they cajoled. Of course I had the wind knocked out of me. Lesson learned about listening to the wrong advice.

When we were five and three, we sang duets at church: "Jesus Wants Me For a Sunbeam", "I've Got a Mansion," "I'll Be Somewhere Listenin' For My Lord", and others. Joyce accompanied us on the piano as we sang. Our sister voices blended together well as we harmonized. Occasionally, though, something funny happened in the audience that caused uncontrollable giggling—such as when a balding, white-haired old man sitting toward the front of the sanctuary blew his nose with a loud honk. We glanced sideways at each other and broke into uncontrollable laughter. Each time we tried to stop the giggling, I'd glance at Eileen, lips quivering, remember the loud honking sound, and we'd burst into gales of laughter once more.

Mom sewed us matching dresses. One of my favorites is featured in a family photo I treasure. The crinkly opaque fabric made crackly sounds when I wore the blouse embossed with white flowers with its rounded collar, trimmed in ruffles. A plaid blue-and-green-jumper with black patent leather shoes and white ruffled socks completed the Christmas outfit. This wasn't the only time we sported new clothes; Mom would sew wardrobe items at Easter and the start of a new school year. Not only did she make dresses and skirts, blouses, and pedal pushers, she sewed thick wool coats. When each girl was a bride, Mother fashioned gowns at a quarter the retail price—perfectly stitched, beautiful, and unique.

Despite getting to show off my lovely, handmade dresses, I was very shy as a young girl. I would speak only if asked a direct question. "What's your name, little girl? Cat got your tongue?"

The Quiring family (Pictured Top L-R: Shirley, Joyce, Dad;
Bottom L-R: Eileen, Mom, Betsy, Roger)

"Shirley Mae Quiring," I'd answer quietly.

Ed was my school bus driver during the seven years I attended Orient Grade School. He was one of the first men I interacted with outside of family. Ed was a dark-haired, mustached man who also served as the school custodian. His "office" was the boiler room. If kids needed something fixed—a bicycle chain reattached, a lunch pail repaired, or a playground swing mended—Ed would take care of it. Sometimes on the bus route, he'd stop by his own place, a five-acre parcel with a rolling lawn where his German shepherds romped: Whitey and Blackie. Whitey was a dark dog, while Blackie was white. That was Ed; always unconventional.

One day, sitting silently as always in the front seat, I watched as a neighbor girl a couple of years older than me got off the bus and said, "Bye, Ed."

Ed looked around and said, "That's the first time she's ever said anything to me!" He was smiling. I thought, *I've been too scared to say anything. If Judy can do it, so can I.* The bus rumbled on its way to my house and I heard the puff and hiss of the air brakes as the bus came to a stop. I got up, gathered my books, scooted to the center aisle and hopped down the steps. Ed slid a lever with a screech and the door opened.

I turned back and looked at Ed. "Bye, Ed!" I shyly said. Ed smiled and with a wink said, "Bye, blondie!" He gave a nod and shut the door.

From that time on, I'd greet him with a "Morning, Ed." In the afternoons it was "Bye, Ed." It felt good. I started raising my hand in class and taking steps to push myself out of my comfort zone.

Besides dealing with painful shyness, I harbored many fears. In our narrow house, the only bathroom was off the kitchen with the light switch at the opposite end of the room. That meant I had to run the gauntlet of the dark, frightening-at-night kitchen to the bathroom before I could hit the light. It was scary to a seven year old—even when my family was in the next room!

"Don't run in the house!" Mama would say. If she only knew how frightened I was of the dark, she wouldn't have said anything.

I always knew I was loved and safe—in spite of those fears that I never expressed to my parents.

The first time we went to an Oregon beach, I was terrified that the waves would keep on coming and cover me with foamy wetness. I hid behind the driftwood. I'd read about tidal waves and, even at home a hundred miles inland, I continued to fear that a tidal wave would sweep us out to sea. I comforted myself that we could run to the church if such disaster loomed.

These unfounded childhood worries evolved into other fears. Some of the things that have terrified me as an adult include attending a job interview, speaking to a group of people, teaching a group of rowdy children in music class, directing an adult choir, leading a women's group, climbing a mountain, learning to fly a small airplane, and rappelling from a tall rock. Yet of all these frightful challenges, facing the death of a loved one was the most terrifying. I was always afraid that one of my parents would die just as my grandma Richert had.

It isn't always easy when I try something the first time, but later it's never as bad or difficult as I thought. Just as I learned to push myself out of my shyness, I've found it rewarding to try new things despite my fears .

Next door to the parsonage was the simple, framed church. Its Gothic windows were built in the late eighteen hundreds and the front door sat up high with at least fifteen steps leading up to it. Every Sunday morning, Dad pulled the belfry rope to ring the bell in the steeple. Inside sat hard, wooden pews and the pulpit, made from a tree stump. Highly varnished, it had a smooth top and showed beautiful grains. A visiting evangelist once remarked that the solid wood hurt his hand as he pounded it during his preaching!

Early Sunday mornings, Dad would kindle a fire in the church basement furnace so the building would be warm. Every week, Dad typed the bulletin and ran it through the mimeograph machine. We children would help fold copies on Saturday afternoons. When Joyce was a teenager, she cleaned the church for a small salary. Sometimes I got to help her dust the pews and she'd pay me; we all participated in some way. Dad's calling was ours, too.

Along with my fears and shyness, I suffered frequent temper tantrums. I felt out of control and wanted *someone* to help me stop—but I didn't know how to communicate that. One morning before school, I put on my favorite mint green dress. It had a lace-up white bodice like something Heidi would have worn in the classic book set in Switzerland. I was surprised when it was much shorter and tighter than the last time I'd worn it. "Shirley, it's too small for you," Mama said at the breakfast table. "You may not wear it."

I shrieked, kicked, and flailed my arms. I wanted to wear that dress. Yet all through that school day, wearing a different dress, I felt a heavy sadness for my earlier behavior. When I came home from school, I said, "I'm sorry, Mama, for having a fit today."

Mom quickly put her arms around me and gave me a kiss. "Of course I forgive you," she said, having already forgotten the tantrum during her busy day.

The sense of anger at a loss of control continues with me today. Tantrums arise when I attempt to use new software on a computer and can't get it to work. I love the navigation system in my car but often want to smash it in frustration when it doesn't accept my input as quickly as I think it should. Sometimes I grumble at other drivers when I think they should move faster.

Stubbornness has positive and negative sides. The positive side showed itself in my life when I didn't give up on my first marriage during difficult times. In the same way, I've been fiercely loyal to friends and family members when they have been in need. Yet the negative side of stubbornness rears its head when I stick to something I believe is right instead of letting it go. Or when I persist in thinking *my* way is the only way.

One morning in my seventh summer, I held my breath with excitement as I lined up for Vacation Bible School. I stood with the other children outside the church, ready to march inside to music from the piano. I'd awakened with a scratchy throat and achy head, but I ignored the sensations. Then my mother bent down to take a close look at me. "Shirley, what are those red blotches on your neck?" She quickly determined I had measles. "You need to go home and go to bed!" Disappointed, I trudged slowly home and put myself to bed. I had been anticipating Bible School for weeks. I knew there'd be stories, snacks, and crafts that I'd miss out on.

I always looked forward to Sunday School and Vacation Bible School was a bonus. It didn't matter that our classrooms were tiny basement rooms with little or no decoration. I loved Bible stories and singing songs about how much Jesus loved me. I memorized Scripture that has stayed with me to this day. Now, reciting verses in my head when I cannot sleep serves me well and gives me wonderful thoughts as I finally drop off to sleep.

Most of the time I'd listen to Dad preach. If I wiggled too much, Mama would pinch me on the leg—hard. I learned to sit still for I knew better than to say "ouch" out loud. Incidentally, I tried pinching my own firstborn when he was too wiggly in church. I realized Mama's technique was just not going to work for me when he loudly said, "Ouch!"

Mama sang alto and sitting beside her, I learned to sing in harmony. When I grew bored, I would gaze at the hymn board that listed the service's hymns, the amount of money in the offering, and the number of children attending Sunday School. I'd make up different words from that hymn board. And even though I didn't listen to every word of the sermons, the message of love and faith entered my head and heart.

Dad preached about weeds. He talked about how a beet leaf has a reddish-green oval shape. Next to it grows a weed that looks similar. It appears *somewhat* like a beet—but instead of an edible root, it bears a long, skinny, stubborn root. He went on to explain how harmful things in our life can crop up, looking good. Beliefs or cults can look similar to the faith but prove slightly off. Misbelief can clog up our life instead of enriching it.

Dad would mention his children in illustrations and it always made me sit up a little straighter to hear my name. I loved my role in our special family.

The Petersons had a comfortable farmhouse with a large, covered porch overlooking a quiet country road. There were church picnics in early summer with potato salad, a freshly butchered fried chicken, and fresh strawberries on top of homemade vanilla ice cream.

Inside, the stone fireplace stood tall as an adult. Rocking chairs flanked the fireplace and the fragrance of wood smoke permeated the walls. Whenever the seven of us arrived for a meal, Mrs. Peterson laid out an assortment of pretty china and we three youngest girls were given child-sized cups and saucers to drink our milk. Best of all, we could run about after dinner, exploring the hayloft in the big barn and peering in on the horse and cows. The pasture held skunk cabbage and the woods were perfect for playing hide-and-seek. Summers meant three-legged races in the nearby pasture. But the word of warning was to watch out for the electric fence. It could send a wicked jolt through your hand.

Many of our after-church dinners were wonderful, such as the ones we shared at the Petersons'—but sometimes there were surprises.

I'll never forget Mr. and Mrs. White. Their one-room house was cozy. The high featherbed stood in one corner of the room with the kitchen set back in an alcove. They had a roomy, unoccupied second house on the property.

"Remember to say please and thank you," Mama said as we drove up. "Whatever you put on your plate, you must eat. Just take a spoonful if you're not sure you like it."

"We will!" we four children chorused from the backseat of the sedan. Betsy, the baby of the family, rode in front with Mama and Daddy.

Mrs. White greeted us at the door. She wore an old-fashioned dress with opaque stockings, her feet in serviceable oxfords with chunky heels. Her gray hair was pulled back in a messy knot. Her high cheekbones were rounded with a spot of red rouge.

She was all ready for us, her dining table set up in the one room. She had fried chicken, mashed potatoes and gravy, home canned green beans, and my favorite: red jello with chunks of pineapple. The crown jewel of the meal was on the counter: a thickly-frosted chocolate cake with three layers. The rich, buttery frosting glistened invitingly.

Mrs. White cleared our plates and brought the cake to the table. "Who would like a piece?" she asked. We all nodded, "Yes, please." We waited in anticipation for our dessert.

"Reverend Quiring?" Mrs. White asked.

"Yes, thank you," he said with a smile. Chocolate was his favorite, though he preferred it in a pie. She carefully cut the first wedge, a nice hefty piece. She cut one side, then the other. Carefully she lifted the tall, triangle-shaped confection and placed it on a plate. We passed the plate to our dad. But what Mrs. White did next took our breaths away. Carefully, she took the cake knife, placed it in her mouth, and quickly zipped it between her lips, cleaning the excess frosting. Taking a napkin, she wiped her mouth. Our family looked at each other, aghast. We knew better than to say anything as she continued her task. Now that the knife was free of frosting, our hostess cut the next piece and looked at Mama.

"Mrs. Quiring?"

Mama cleared her throat and said, as graciously as possible, "Yes, I'd love a piece. Thank you."

Each time Mrs. White cut a piece, she licked the knife. Each of us was given our slice of cake. Somehow we finished dessert. But we have never forgotten that day.

Mrs. White liked me. I'm not sure why. Was I a reminder of herself at age ten, a quiet blonde girl? They were childless—maybe she'd always dreamed of having a daughter. There were five children present at the dinner, yet it was me she invited to stay after the dinner was over. "Would it be all right if Shirley stayed for the rest of the afternoon?" she asked after the dishes were put away. "She can ride back with us to church service tonight."

Please, please, Mama. Say no! I pleaded inwardly. I didn't want to be there all by myself! What would I say to them?

"That would be all right," Mama answered. The rest of the family drove down the long, graveled driveway and left me with a lump in my throat.

I wandered the yard. I peeked in the larger house, walked through it, and peered through the dirty windows. Mrs. White gave me an ice cream cookie for a treat—thankfully, she didn't do anything weird to contaminate it, and there was no more chocolate cake. Somehow, we got through that very strange afternoon.

Mr. Ainsley was a bachelor. At every Sunday service and Wednesday night prayer meeting, he would sit on the left-hand side in the middle of the long, hardwood pews. In those days, everyone wore their Sunday best. For the men, it was the only time they dressed up; this meant a suit, white shirt, and tie. They were berry growers in overalls, laborers at the nearby sawmill, or workers in the cannery. Mr. Ainsley was the janitor at a local business.

He was a short man with a few sparse white hairs on his head. He seemed the splitting image of Blimpy from the Popeye cartoons—the character who couldn't resist hamburgers and ate piles of them. He had a large stomach that his suit coat very nearly covered. He wore a hat, which he hung on the hat tree in the narthex.

Several times a year, there would be an all-church potluck, which meant lots of good food to a bachelor who most likely ate his meals from a can. Mr. Ainsley would pile a plate you'd think would topple over with mashed potatoes and gravy, macaroni and cheese, hamburger pie, and—of course—Swedish meatballs from the Scandinavian families. He couldn't get enough.

After consuming all of his dinner, he returned to the dessert table that sat groaning under the ladies' best. Apple crisp, lemon meringue pie, German chocolate cake. When he returned to his one-room house out in the country, I'm sure he slept with a satisfied smile on his face.

One Sunday, Leo Cadwin, a deacon and friend of Mr. Ainsley, approached my Dad. "Reverend Quiring, Jack Ainsley isn't at church today. He's never missed a service."

Sure enough, Mr. Ainsley was very ill. After checking on him, church members took him to the hospital where he died after a few days. Though he didn't have any family by his bed, his church family was with him.

In heaven, surely he enjoys pleasures greater than the heaped plates of food he looked forward to those few times each year.

The Ford Model A coupe rattled into the gravel-lined parking lot at the country church. A man who looked like Ichabod Crane sat at the wheel. An enormous woman in a tent-like dress was in the passenger seat next to him. Joe parked near the front steps and walked around in a bent position to open the woman's door. Greta eased out of the car, pulling herself up with the help of the strap on the door. She grasped the handrail as she lumbered up the fifteen steps, greeting those next to her and nodding her head, showcasing a double chin and a neck as large as a football lineman. Her flat shoes rolled to the side because of her great weight.

Greta was a great aunt to our neighborhood friends and Joe a divorcé.

Joe was Greta's handyman, living in a room off of the garage—not in the house with her. He tended the grounds where she grew strawberries and raspberries. He maintained her machinery and kept that Model A in tip-top condition. Perhaps they had breakfast together, discussing the jobs that needed to be done or the weather for the day.

Greta and Joe loved each other very much. But with Joe's ex-wife still living, he believed he was not free to marry. Some might think their Bible interpretation too strict but they believed it was right.

All of these characters in our little country church had their own sorrows, joys, and histories. As a child, I felt enriched by them all.

CHAPTER 13

VIOLINS, BERRIES, AND BABIES

"Maturity is when your world opens up and
you realize you are not the center of it."
—M.J. Croan

One morning at school, my second-grade teacher Mrs. Swaren announced "a wonderful opportunity" for those of us who wanted to learn an instrument.

Excitedly, I told the family at the dinner table about the possibility of playing violin. Both parents asked, "Would you be willing to practice every day?"

"Oh yes!" I squealed. I loved music. Soon I was enrolled in group lessons with a three-quarter sized violin and a lesson book. I loved the beautifully-shaped instrument and learned how to care for all of its parts. It was a beautiful violin case with an outside of fake alligator skin and a velvet lining of deep burgundy.

I learned patriotic songs, Christmas carols, and folk tunes by Stephen Foster. Our teacher, an excellent violinist from Scotland, showed us how to draw the bow carefully across the strings without wandering from the bridge. After several months, Mr. Ewart told my mother and Mrs. Fredericks that Toni and I were progressing much quicker than the other students. He offered to teach us separately for two dollars per week.

Mr. Ewart would come to Toni's home early before classes began and give our thirty minute lesson before driving us to school. He used old teaching techniques, raising his voice to scold us in frustration. Even so, he fueled the desire to please. I felt that if I could play like him, it would be a dream come true.

Together, Toni and I played duets at school, and I performed solos at church with Joyce accompanying me on the piano.

When I was ten, I asked if I could take piano lessons, too. Since money was tight, Mom took over the task, teaching me and Eileen. She arranged recitals so we could dress up, host friends, and invite our grandparents from nearby Dallas. After we played the piano and violin pieces learned especially for the day, Mom served cookies and punch.

Our parents offered amazing support for our musical talents. They set aside any extra money for private lessons. They listened to Eileen and I as we harmonized on road trips or sang duets in our adult years. Joyce played the pump organ at church and had all the makings of an accomplished musician. When Dad needed to identify a new song to teach to the congregation, he'd hum the melody and she would play it by ear.

Every evening after dinner, our family would gather in the living room for devotions. We would read a passage from the Bible together. Each person read two verses until we completed the chapter. When it was my turn, I hoped the verses would be long ones, for I loved reading out loud. After we finished the reading, we'd discuss the chapter and kneel by the sofa to pray. A few months before the last member of our family was born, requests centered around the baby.

"Dear Jesus, please be with Mama and the baby," I prayed. "And please let it be a boy so Roger has a playmate."

"God may not bring us a boy," Daddy reminded us.

"You mean, even though Roger wants a boy, we don't have to pray for one?" I asked.

"No."

"Oh, goody!" I breathed. "I really wanted a baby sister!" From that point on, I prayed for a girl.

It was a hot July day. We sat in the front yard on the porch, waiting for the news. Soon we saw the 1950 lime green Pontiac drive down the gravel road, sunlight flashing on the windshield. "What did Mama have?" we chorused as Daddy stepped from the car.

"Well, you have a new baby sister," he answered carefully. "I know you might be disappointed, Roger." My brother's face dropped in disappointment and his shoulders slumped. But then his face brightened. "What will we name her?"

"How does Elizabeth Rose sound?" Perhaps the recent coronation of Queen Elizabeth was in the back of Daddy's mind. "We'll call her Betsy for short."

When the tiny, sweet infant arrived at home, I would quietly slip through our closet into the adjoining bedroom to admire her in the little bassinet. I wanted to pick her up but knew I'd get in trouble if I woke her.

At age seven, I learned to change diapers and rock Betsy. In fact, everyone in our church wanted to care for her. She was the darling.

Money was tight that summer so Mom began picking berries. We worked alongside her while Roger babysat Betsy. It was tough getting up so early in the chilly mornings and I fought back sleep. It helped that those freshly picked berries were delicious right off of the vine. I'd pick some and then eat some. Birds warbled their songs and the sounds echoed in the nearby forest.

When the farmer handed me my pay at the end of a season, I had enough to buy my first bike. Meanwhile, Mom, who was quick with her hands, had picked enough strawberries to purchase a much-needed clothes dryer.

Pampered Betsy got to sit in the front seat of the sedan while the rest of the five kids wrestled for "our spot" in the back seat. But she was a joy. We laughed when she substituted "shurch" for church and "po" for her favorite pillow.

Fourteen years older, Joyce was Betsy's second mother. She was the one Betsy ran to if she was hurting. When Joyce went to college, she missed Betsy most.

My childhood might sound idyllic and I think it was. We roamed the countryside, explored the woods, and learned to run and ride bicycles as fast as the wind on country roads without the danger of cars. Deserted chicken coops made perfect theaters to produce plays for pretend audiences.

Roger was always relegated to a funky, unfinished room in the early years. Rather than deprive him, it helped make him self-sufficient. He was the one sibling who never had to share a room.

One hot summer day, the tarred road looked like an undulating piece of black licorice, soft because of the heat. Roger, Ernie, and I zipped down the road on our bikes.

I was so proud of my bike, bought with berry-picking money. It wasn't brand new but it was big—a twenty-six incher—with large balloon tires. Dad had painted it a dusty rose, my chosen color, and I'd bought a new seat and rubber handgrips.

We were going around "the corner": the steepest part of the meandering curve that had no shoulder except for a few inches of sharp rock. It was so steep that Ed would honk the school bus horn as we slowly descended, warning oncoming traffic to watch for the bus filled with children.

Sunshine dappled the winding road as we descended. It was difficult to see the freshly tarred surface and the gravel on top of the asphalt. Ernie passed me just as we were approaching the corner. I moved to the shoulder to avoid a collision and my tires skidded wildly. I flipped off the bike, scraping arms and knees.

Bloody, I picked myself up. The tears flowed when I looked at my new bike seat and saw the scrape on the back side.

"Pick up the bike, Ernie," Roger commanded in an annoyed, stern voice. Ernie, dressed in scruffy pants with one leg rolled up to prevent bike chain tangles, hurriedly threw his bike to the side of the road and picked up mine. He pushed it home as the two boys walked, trailed by a bedraggled, sobbing girl with bloody knees, her nose runny from crying. Roger looked back every few minutes to check on me. It's one of my strongest memories of Roger showing me his love.

As for that bike, it served me my whole childhood and I didn't get another until my twenties. The scraped seat became a badge of honor of my toughness.

Despite the moments of love, there were many strained occasions with my brother. In future summers picking berries, he'd tease me because I "scooted" my berry carrier alongside the berry row. "Shirley the scooter," he'd mimic in a singsong voice.

I'd whine and fume. "No, I'm not!"

"Yes, you are. Shirley the scooter! Ha, ha!" he crowed.

"Leave me alone!" I cried.

Once he put baby garter snakes in my handlebars. *That's* why I don't like snakes! But looking back, those times when he picked on me gave me courage to stand up for myself when necessary.

The upright piano, the pump organ, and the acoustics of unadorned wooden walls and hard wooden pews encouraged lusty, enthusiastic singing. There were voiced Amens when Daddy would make a point in his sermon. Such was the worship in those early days at the Baptist church. Words to those hymns still ring in my head, bringing me comfort at difficult times in my life.

> Blessed assurance
> Jesus is mine
> Oh, what a foretaste of Glory Divine!
> Heir of Salvation, purchase of God,
> Born of His spirit, washed in His blood.[8]

My favorite Easter song, then and now, reminds me of Easter lilies and daffodils carefully placed by children onto a moss-covered cross. I see organdy dresses with full petticoats, girls with white gloves, brand new shoes, and ruffled socks.

> Christ the Lord is risen today,
> Alleluia!
> Sons of men and angels say
> Alleluia![9]

Sunday nights meant church meetings, too. The arched windows were open during the summer to let the cool evening breeze flow in the building. I would gaze out at those open windows and watch the night sky as it turned from blue to darker blue, deep purple, and finally black velvet. I felt like crying as we sang the gospel hymn.

> Just as I am without one plea
> But that Thy blood was shed for me,
> And that Thou bidd'st me come to Thee,
> O Lamb of God, I come!
> I come![10]

I knew even at that young age how much I needed my Savior to keep me close. One evening after the service, I ran home, knelt down by my bed, and once again asked Jesus to come into my heart. He was already there but I needed the assurance again.

Mom used her artistry to present Bible stories in Sunday School and Vacation Bible School. I never grew tired of the stories she told with pictures—her "chalk talks." She set up a large easel with an array of thick, colored chalk. When the lights lowered, Mom sketched a scene while music played in the background: a recording of a poem, an inspirational story, or a Bible passage she narrated. Sometimes the scene was a beach, a mountain, or country church in a valley. Or she might depict the Holy Land with stucco square houses, rooftop patios, and palm trees. The pictures would come to life and the audience would "ooh and ahh" as she drew. Then the lights switched off and Mom would turn on the black lights. All of a sudden, the pictures would change from pastels to radiant neons, with lit windows and pathways previously unseen. Mom continued this magical chalk artistry all of her life, even in the retirement home where she lived her last days.

At the close of each service, Daddy would lead the congregation to the chorus of song.

> God be with you till we meet again;
> By His counsels guide, uphold you,
> With His sheep securely fold you,
> God be with you till we meet again.[11]

He closed with a benediction.

May the grace of the Lord Jesus Christ, and the love of God, the Father, and fellowship of the Holy Spirit be with you all.

It was a comfort to hear those words. And hurrah! We didn't have to sit still anymore. We played outside until it was time for Mama's Sunday dinner of roast pork or fried chicken with mashed potatoes and gravy, homemade applesauce, and home canned green beans or corn—with pie for dessert.

Home had its rewards and benefits. It's true that living in a pastor's home was sometimes like living in a glass house. A box of Red Delicious apples might be dropped by our back door—a gift from a church member's orchard. At other times, visitors would come inside and the house needed to be neat and clean. We couldn't leave dishes dirty or beds unmade. We hosted visiting missionaries and evangelists, and we all learned to converse at the dinner table as well as listen to words of wisdom and interesting stories.

I learned that every decision I made could affect my dad and his position as a spiritual leader in the community. Sometimes I would let an argument go with a friend whose dad was a deacon—just to avoid bad feelings. As a teenager I turned down party or drinking invitations. There seemed a higher standard for us and it helped me choose the best way of working out a conflict.

I still did my share of mischief. Once, an evangelist who performed magic tricks visited. Eileen and I sneaked into the church where he kept his props. We examined all his magic paraphernalia, figuring out how he performed each trick. After learning the secrets, all the fun was lost.

As siblings, we'd fight tooth and nail. If our fists hit a little too hard, a quick "I'm sorry, sorry, sorry!" would follow to avoid our parent's wrath.

The parsonage was just across the driveway and Dad's office in the church building. I rushed across the parking lot with requests. Some of those trips across the driveway were spurred by a homework question when my mother was too busy to help or a need for Dad to type a report. One afternoon I had a special request. "Can I go to the movies with Susan and Karen on Friday night. Please?"

"You know we don't go to movies, Shirley," Dad answered.

"But it's Cinderella. And it's in technicolor!" I said earnestly, building my case to attend a movie theater for the first time.

My dad hid his smile. "Well, maybe we can make an exception." He looked at me seriously. "How are you going to pay for it?"

"I have my allowance saved up. Maybe I can do an extra job for the last dollar I need."

"All right," he grinned.

Whenever the urge struck, we could run to that church building to play ping-pong, scurry up and down the stairs, or start games of hide-and-seek. In winter, the cold didn't stop us. I tried every pump organ in every building. Of course, the best one was in the sanctuary. We could sing solos in a bright, operatic style with only the empty room as our audience. We might preach a sermon imagining the pews filled with congregation members.

There was only one telephone in our house, on a small desk in the dining room. The church did not have one. Dad rigged up an intercom system with two old-fashioned telephones, the kind with handheld earpieces. *Ring, ring, ring*, the old timey bell rang out when I turned the hand crank. "Yes?" Daddy's would come across the telephone line connecting our house to his study at the church.

"Mr. Peterson is on the phone; he wants to speak with you," I'd say, standing on tiptoe as I spoke into the mouthpiece.

"I'll be right there. Tell him to hold on," Daddy would say. The back door slammed as he rushed into the house. "Hello, Harley . . . yes, yes. I understand. We'll get someone to substitute for your class tomorrow . . ." My parents were careful to not share details, for there were nine parties using the same phone line. That meant that any one of the party members could pick up the phone and listen to the conversation. Often there were very personal things shared with a pastor and his wife. These people were part of God's work and confidential conversations were kept in confidence.

At the same time, we were the first to know whenever there was a birth, death, or illness in the congregation. The church members were our extended family and we cared about them. And nothing was more thrilling than to hear from Dad that someone had become a Christian.

Challenges of young childhood seemed complicated to me at age ten, but dealing with a teasing brother, negotiating new privileges with a parent, and learning to play an instrument were just a platform for handling life's complications later on.

CHAPTER 14

THE RELATIONSHIP DEEPENS

"God gave us everything in pairs: two hands, two
eyes, two ears . . . but why only one heart? Because
he gave another to someone else to go find."
—Unknown

"I think I'd like to attend one more session of GriefShare," Jim
said as we met for dinner one evening.

"A new session starts tomorrow night," I answered.

"Would you mind if I came to it?"

"Of course not!" I tried not to sound too excited but I was
singing inside. *He wants to be with me. He wants to know more about
me. Goody, goody!*

"How about I pick something up to eat before the meeting and
drive us?"

"Sure," I said nonchalantly. The night of the meeting, Jim
brought a Caesar salad with with veggies and chicken which we
ate quickly before heading to the church.

I went to work, setting up for the GriefShare meeting. I hoped
there would be plenty of participants in this program. It was so
instrumental in helping a person move through grief. My friend
Jane arrived to help me set out books and heat water for tea. She
too was a widow. We had been friends since junior high and became
close after we lost our husbands about a year apart.

There were six of us when we started the meeting. Besides Jane,
there was another widow, a twenty-something girl whose mother
died suddenly, a widower, and a daughter who hadn't grieved the

death of her mother forty years earlier. And then there was Jim. He mentioned that a "friend" had told him about the gathering.

I listened, my heart breaking, as Jim described losing his thirty-one-year-old daughter to sleep apnea. Less than three years later, his wife Kathy died after a long struggle with pulmonary fibrosis.

While leading the class, I tried not to give too much attention to Jim. He was trying to be very careful, too. I glanced at him from time to time, loving the serious look on his face. He listened sympathetically and nodded when Hal, the widower, told how lonely he was. I was falling in love with this caring man and I'd known him less than a week!

"You did a fantastic job leading the group!" Jim enthused as we drove out of the parking lot. "You are a natural."

My heart beat faster at the warm compliment. I smiled at him.

It was getting late and I had a series of speaking engagements beginning the following morning. I didn't want to say good night. We continued our conversation at home on my couch, our backs to opposite armrests and our feet entwined as we talked quietly about each other's lives. Jim would hug me from time to time or kiss me on the cheek. After about an hour, he kissed me again on the cheek and I said, "When are you going to give me a *real* kiss?"

That's all it took. He leaned forward and gave me a real kiss, full of passion. After a bit, he looked up. "Shirley, I *love* you."

"I love you, too!" I quickly responded, surprised by my answer.

The connection was amazing. "Only a week or so ago, I asked God to bring someone into my life who would want to be with me," I told him. "I prayed for God to 'drop him in my lap.' "

Jim stood up, turned around, and *sat* right on my lap! We laughed with joy.

All too soon, Jim said, "I know you have to get up early, Shirley. I'll get going."

I sighed, knowing he was right, as I had to make a hundred-mile drive in the morning. "I'm so glad you came tonight."

"I am, too." He hesitated a moment. "I'd like to hear your talk. Would it be possible? I'll stay in the back of the room." We made plans to meet later in the week so he could hear me tell my story in a small logging town near Olympia.

Just as he promised, Jim slipped into the back of the Mexican restaurant at Yelm to listen. After the meeting, we found a cafe nearby. Summer was making her last blast of heat before fall began and we were grateful for the air conditioning as we ordered appetizers and iced tea.

I glanced around the restaurant. Two rugged, old men wearing blue denim shirts and bright red suspenders sat in a booth, deep in conversation—perhaps of past logging days. A single man pored over paperwork, groomed like a salesman with shirt and tie askew. How could they sit there, unaware of the excitement we were experiencing with each other?

We sat, wishing time would stop. Something big was happening in our lives. We held hands across the table. Soon though, I needed to drive to my next speaking destination.

"You've told me about living in Portland and in the country. What about middle and high school?"

"Well, in the middle of seventh grade, my dad got a phone call . . ."

CHAPTER 15

MOVING TO WASHINGTON

"This is my country; God gave it to me; I will protect it, ever
keep it free. Small towns and cities rest here in the sun,
Filled with our laughter, 'Thy will be done.'"
—Helen Davis, *Washington State song*

"Yes. Thank you. God bless you, too." Dad was speaking to the chairman of the pastoral search committee for Brush Prairie Baptist Church. The church had unanimously voted to hire him as pastor of their southwest Washington congregation.

"Yeah!" we all shouted—and the new adventure began.

In Oregon, I had been near the top of the heap as a seventh grader at my eight-grade elementary school. In Battle Ground, I was at the bottom. I had multiple teachers, PE (with showers), "math" instead of arithmetic, and a locker combination to memorize. Best of all, we had a library instead of a visiting bookmobile. The shelves were full of old favorites alongside books I'd never seen before. I loved mysteries and reading about characters like student nurse Sue Barton and detective Nancy Drew.

After lunch, there were paths to wander. We strolled past the ivy-covered two-story brick building, enjoying the sun-dappled paths, chatting with friends, and flirting with boys.

Music had grown to be an important part of my life. Eileen and I still sang duets together and I was flattered when church friends Debbie and Judy invited me to sing with them in a group called The Teenettes. We sang gospel songs in three-part harmony, performing at churches in the area, Baptist regional youth meetings, and Bible camp.

When I wasn't singing, studying, or helping at home, I was spending time with our big, lively youth group, made up of kids from several school districts. We'd gather together on Friday nights after basketball and football games, eating or playing shuffleboard and ping-pong. We'd laugh and flirt, surrounded by a crowd of peers.

Meanwhile, things were changing at home. Joyce married and Roger joined the Navy. I took over as the oldest in the nest, looking after Eileen and Betsy.

It was about this time I witnessed a death I've never forgotten. Our cat Shiver gave birth to a litter of kittens in the flowering, yellow St. John's Wort next to the house. When we saw Shiver away from her babies, we'd pick her up and firmly return her to them, but she would always scamper away, refusing to care for them. Instinctively, she knew they had a sickness, as one by one, the kittens died until only one was left—Tiger, a tiny tabby who could barely open his eyes. Determined to save him, I fed Tiger milk with a doll bottle, kept him warm, and cuddled him. I *willed* that kitten to live. Still, he continued to sink into himself until at last he died. That day, I learned death cannot be stopped.

My best friend Karen was a bright-eyed girl who lived just down the road and got straight As. We read together, studied together, and had sleepovers. We fixed our hair and I loaned her my makeup since she wasn't allowed any at home. We sang together in our ensemble, gave each other rides to games and performances, and I taught her to drive a stick shift. We shared our hopes—her desire to be a teacher, mine to be a nurse—as well as our dreams of marriage.

After graduation, we continued to be best friends. At eighteen years old, we felt invincible, with our lives in front of us. I attended Clark College and worked as a sales clerk at Meier & Frank, a department store in Portland.

"Shirley, sit down. I need to tell you something," Mom said one cold, wintry evening. I was returning from an evening shift. *Am I in trouble?* I wondered. I needed to get to my room to finish a paper for English class and yet I could hear the concern in Mom's voice.

Mom turned up the television volume and I heard a voice on the ten o'clock news.

"Karen Rose Schlecht has died from head injuries sustained in a head-on collision on Union Avenue in Portland." The voice droned on but the words stunned me. My mind could scarcely take it in. Mom took me in her arms and I sobbed, unable to fully comprehend the loss.

Next day, in the restroom at Clark College, two friends from my high school class were talking. "*Shhh*," Vicki said to Donna. She didn't want me to hear the discussion of my best friend's death, thinking it would hurt more. I ignored them and their hushed conversation. I couldn't acknowledge the wrenching loss, afraid I'd break down and cry.

It was my first experience with the death of someone close. I had a difficult time believing that it had happened, but when I saw her shattered body in the coffin a few days later, I knew it was so.

I remembered a conversation I'd had with my mother about her own grieving. "I wanted so badly to talk about my mama," she said as she washed and rinsed a dinner plate, handing it to me.

"Why didn't you?" I asked, as I slowly dried the plate with the towel.

"They thought it would hurt me if we talked about her," Mom said, shaking her head.

I had learned with the kitten that I could not prevent death using my own will. And at eighteen, I learned we are fragile human beings. Death will not be stopped.

CHAPTER 16

BILL: THE EARLY YEARS

"Marriage: Love is the reason. Lifelong friendship is the gift.
Kindness is the cause. Till death do us part is the length."
—Fawn Weaver

Jim and I had been sitting at the restaurant for over an hour. "Boy, you do have wonderful memories," Jim said, squeezing my hand. He glanced at his watch, "I know you have to drive to the coast this afternoon, but do you have time to tell me about you and Bill? How did you meet?"

"Oh yes," I said, leaning back into the booth, enjoying the warmth of his shoulder next to mine. I was sixteen, going on seventeen . . ."

"Who is that blonde? I want to meet her!" Bill was chatting with his brother's girlfriend at a youth group birthday party. I had dashed into the room, chasing a balloon. Unaware that they were talking about me, I retrieved my balloon and ran out.

The following Sunday, Bill and I were both attending an event with multiple church youth groups. There was lots of singing, a devotional given by the youth leader, and of course, food. As fifty teenagers stood around, munching on sandwiches and eyeing anyone of the opposite sex, Bill sidled up to me.

"Hi, I don't think we've met. My name is Bill Rudberg. I hear that you're Pastor Quiring's daughter." Being the pastor's daughter could be scary to a potential suitor but Bill smiled confidently, showing off his large, straight teeth and friendly hazel eyes.

"Hello," I said nervously, surprised he had noticed me. We chatted about the weather and insignificant things, just to keep the conversation going. I liked his confidence and maturity.

Bill was six feet tall with curly, dark brown hair. He was broad-chested with a strong body. At nineteen, this California boy had a car: a four-door, gray and white 1956 Chevy hardtop with dual pipes that gave it a throaty, deep sound. What more could a girl want?

He was the new guy in town and he wasn't afraid to ask a girl out. "Would you like to go out with me next Saturday? There's a concert at Columbia River High School. We could go to Shakey's Pizza afterwards."

"Uh, sure," I said with surprise.

Our relationship moved quickly after that first date. Though I was normally shy around boys, I felt totally comfortable with him. We couldn't stop talking. He waited until our third date to kiss me—and I was ready for that kiss. After that evening, I floated into the house with the memory. Soon we were a couple. I couldn't wait to be with Bill every minute of every day and night.

I still remember those tummy-fluttery times, even more than fifty years later. It wasn't long before we were talking about marriage. "How'd you like to be married to a cop?" he asked.

"I would like to be married to a cop—or to any other profession. Just as long as you're the one!" I said with a smile. We hugged and kissed each other happily. We became officially engaged after high school. His graduation gift was a solitaire diamond ring set in white gold.

Dad officiated on a hot July evening one year later. The newspaper described my gown as

> a full length sheath of Alencon lace fashioned with bodice of silk organza with bateau neckline and long sleeves coming to points over the hands. Her elbow veil was held in place by a tiara of seed pearls and her bridal bouquet was a cascade of yellow rosebuds and stephanotis tied with white satin ribbons.

Bill and Shirley Rudberg on July 16, 1965.

The celebration was full of family. Two of my sisters served as bridesmaids. Bill's brother Don served as best man. Roger was an usher, and Betsy, a candle lighter.

In the fall, I started the nursing program at Clark College. Bill was an apprentice in a machine shop, having completed his Associate in Applied Science at Clark. In two years, he would finish his apprenticeship and become a Journeyman Machinist. A quick learner, Bill soon mastered many different machines.

We were busy those first years. I worked part-time and went to classes full-time. Bill worked full-time on swing shift and took classes in the morning. We'd rush home after school and I'd make a quick dinner in time for Bill to go to his job at Columbia Machine.

Our first home was ready for us when we returned from a three-day honeymoon. It was a two-bedroom cottage; one wall was nearly all glass and rustic, dark beams framed the high ceilings.

Two weeks after our wedding, I planned a bridal shower for Debbie, one of my best friends. That hot August afternoon, I heard the car pull into the driveway. "I'm home!" Bill said, giving me a hug and kiss. He was working dayshift that particular week. I scurried around the house, picking things up, cleaning the kitchen counter, and making some punch. "What's for dinner?" he asked.

"Uh, dinner?" I had been so busy planning the party, working a full day at a retail dress shop in Portland, and then hurrying home to get things ready. "There's no dinner tonight," I said. "I'm sorry, I forgot to make something. I'm getting ready for the shower for Debbie. And by the way, you need to be gone. The house will be full of women."

"Shower? What?! You didn't tell me!" He swore. "What am I supposed to do?"

"Well, can't you go to your mom's?" I asked anxiously. A wave of guilt came over me for failing to communicate. I covered it with defensiveness. *What's the matter with him? I forgot to tell him—so what? I just want my girlfriends to see my new home.*

"What if I don't go to Mom's? I'm tired; I've worked all day in that hot shop. I thought I could just relax tonight." He stomped angrily into the bedroom to change his clothes, brushing past me and slamming the door.

Later, he came home to the last few guests who were helping clean up. I pretended everything was fine—until everyone left. Then I turned a cold shoulder to him. *He should apologize, after all!* But I never could give the silent treatment for very long and soon everything seemed to be normal. But the crazy cycle had begun.

Though we were happy together—Christians attending church regularly—we began living more independent lives, a gradual slide into separateness. Yet when we first met, I hadn't even wanted to say goodnight to him. I wish I could say that we figured out how to love and respect each other, but that wouldn't be honest. We were immature and selfish. We lived as single people sharing the same residence—married singles. I did things my way without considering what he might like or want, not realizing we had a home together. He got upset. I got upset. My impulse was to get away from his anger or yell back. This continued for more than twenty years, sad to say. Of course, we had good times between those arguments and yelling sprees. Yet it wasn't how I'd dreamed marriage would be when I took those rose-colored vows.

In between every bout of fighting, we'd try to patch things up and live at peace.

Bill decided he wanted to race our sports car. In order to do that, he needed to add a roll bar and other safety features.

"How much longer do I need to hold this?" I whined as I leaned over the car, holding the bar in place for him to install.

"I just need to tighten the bolts one more time and I think I'm done," Bill said.

An MG Midget with a rag top, it was a sporty car that whizzed around the streets easily. Both of us loved to drive it, but the car wasn't safe without that piece of equipment. Bill planned to race the car in keeping with the standards of the Sports Car Club of America. The roll bar and military aircraft-style seatbelt were requirements.

It was a late February night and I was freezing in our unheated garage. I had get up early for my classes next morning. I waited with impatience while I heard the final clicking of the ratchet wrench and Bill said, "Okay, I'm done. You can go in now."

The next evening, I dropped by my parents' home while Bill worked the night shift. We'd watched *The Andy Griffith Show* until it was time to go home to my studies.

"Thanks for stopping by," Mom called as I closed the door. I hopped into the car with Mike, my black miniature poodle, snapped the seatbelt and was on my way. It was dark and the MG was the only car on the backcountry road. As I was speeding my way home, road barricades suddenly loomed in front of me. I swerved left and the sensitive steering of the MG jerked the car toward the right, swinging me out of control. Before I could react, I was in the front yard of a house with the car flipped. I could hear the clacking of the fuel pump in my ear, the engine still running and not getting the gas it needed. I shakily turned the car off, looking around to place where I was—upside down, hanging from the top of the car and firmly strapped in my seatbelt.

I couldn't move my knee. The fear of being trapped erupted from me with a scream. After a moment, I realized all I had to do was unhook myself. I flipped the three prongs of the seatbelt, yanked my knee loose from where it was stuck against the steering wheel, and dropped down onto the top of the car. Disoriented, I felt for the handle and pushed open the door.

Everything was opposite what it should be. I heard voices and the sound of a siren as I crawled out. I stood up and looked at the car's upside-down-ness, resting on the front lawn beside a telephone pole. *What will I tell Bill?* was my first thought.

Later, we were told I'd have broken my neck and died had that roll bar not been installed just twenty-four hours earlier.

As it turned out, some teenagers had put road barricades in the middle of the road as a prank. After reading about my accident in the newspaper, the teens' parents came forward and paid for a new windshield, the only damage to the car. The only other effects were a large bruise on my knee and a scared poodle.

Dad remarked about the scene after the accident. It had looked like no one could have survived in that tiny, upturned car. Had he not heard my voice on the phone asking him to pick me up, he would have thought they'd be picking out my coffin.

Bill had installed those safety precautions a mere twenty-four hours before the encounter with the road barricades. I'm so grateful for God's protection that kept me from death more than fifty years ago, all because Bill made the choice to add a single piece of equipment.

Bill continued to pursue his hobbies and interests. For a while, it was racing that MG and learning to fly an airplane. He was a natural pilot and instructor; eventually he began to teach at fixed-base flight school in Vancouver. Though he enjoyed working with student pilots, he was frustrated. "I really want to be in the left seat," he told me, "not in the right, correcting other people's mistakes." The instructor job didn't pay very well and he was discouraged and quit his goal of becoming a commercial pilot. As an alternative, he toyed with the idea of joining the military to fly jets, which would have taken him to Vietnam.

He was a natural pilot but, after two years of a salary that barely paid the bills, he went back to his job as a Journeyman Machinist. It wasn't easy. Bill would come home, bored and grumpy from toiling away with the same old equipment in that hot shop. I stood by, feeling helpless, wanting Bill to find fulfillment. He eventually rediscovered a zest for life through his hobbies and continued to add new skills all the time. He rode motorcycles, fished, and learned photography. He became an expert in each new hobby he pursued. After he became competent, he'd move on to something new.

We were married a little more than two years when my friend Darlene visited with her baby girl. She was so cute and little and I loved babies. After they left, I said to Bill, "Please, please can we have a baby?" What could he say to that? Here was his wife, she wanted a baby—and maybe they could start making it right now! He was ready for sex anytime and so I stopped taking the pill right then.

We decided to skip dinner before we left for work, and very soon, we were pregnant. I highly recommend having more conversation about a decision so dramatic and life-changing. Yet neither of us were sorry. I couldn't wait to hold my own baby in my arms!

CHAPTER 17

AND BABY MAKES THREE: TODD WILLIAM

"A mother's love for her child is like nothing else in the world. It knows no law, no pity. It dares all things and crushes down remorselessly all that stands in its path."
—Agatha Christie

I dropped out of nursing school and worked the night shift at a bank in downtown Portland. Bill worked swing shift with the same hours as mine. We were night owls, not going to bed until two or three in the morning, usually watching Johnny Carson's late night show to wind down after work. We used my paycheck to save up for hospital expenses and new furniture for our house and nursery.

Nine months passed quickly and I kept a journal during my pregnancy, avidly read any book I could about child development. I felt confident, facing labor for the first time. After all, I'd studied and witnessed the birth process many times during my nursing classes. In the nursing practicums at Bess Kaiser Hospital, we instructed the young mothers to say "contractions" rather than labor "pains."

In those days, the father stayed with his wife in the labor room, but every time the nurse checked the mother, he would be asked to leave. In her busyness, the nurse often forgot to tell the father he could return. I said to Bill in frustration, "Ask the nurse to let you back into the room." I didn't like being alone in labor and was shocked the contractions hurt as much as they did. I thought back to my nursing practice and my instruction to the mothers. *What a joke. This hurts! It is painful!*

Four hours later, our son was born. When they put him in my arms, he was alert and looked at me quizzically as if to say, "What's up, Mom?" Bill proudly strutted the halls, so glad he had the boy he wanted. Back in my room, we thought of people to call and tell the wonderful news that our baby boy, Todd William, had arrived.

Todd was a delightful, bright baby. In six weeks I'd convinced him he didn't need to wake up in the middle of the night for his four-hour feeding. He was happy, contented, and cute. By the time he was four months old, we decided that I needed to go back to work to help purchase an airplane. The extra flight time Bill logged in a plane of his own would make his credentials more acceptable. I hated leaving my baby in the care of our babysitter but felt I didn't I have a choice. I groused as *she* was the one who watched him take his first baby steps. *She* comforted him when he cried.

Every afternoon, I'd drop Todd off with the babysitter and drive to my nighttime job at the bank, processing checks. A few hours later, Bill would pick up eight-month-old Todd and drive to the airport where they flew until dark in our Taylor Craft two-place airplane.

Bill belted Todd next to him with the carrier on the bench seat and the two of them roared into the sky. Todd had flight time drilled early into his bones—later he and Bill built an airplane together that Todd now flies expertly.

He enjoyed attention from both families as he grew. An inquisitive boy, Todd watched his daddy take cars apart in the garage. He drove the boat when Bill fished for salmon commercially. Even so, it was hard for a ten-year-old. Bill had high expectations and thought Todd should be able to do things right the first time. They got up before dawn and fished all day. As Todd grew, they pursued other hobbies: backpacking, hunting, and sport fishing.

We encouraged Todd to participate in Little League, soccer, and school sports. He took trumpet lessons and played in the marching and jazz bands in high school. Sometimes he'd play in church and I'd accompany him on the piano, reveling in the joy of making music together.

His grades in school didn't reflect how bright he truly was. Teachers would say, "Todd has much more potential than his grades show" or "Todd could turn in his homework more often." We all battled for Todd to turn his homework in. He would say, "Why should I turn in homework when I can ace the tests?" or "It's so boring, waiting for the other kids to get the problem." It was frustrating for all of us.

After graduating from high school, Todd attended the local community college, killing time. One evening, we had a serious discussion. Bill raised his voice in frustration and said, "You either need to start improving your grades or get a job and move out!" Of course, my mother's heart didn't want to hear him say that but I knew he was right. Bill continued, "I think you should join the military until you know what you want to do!"

Todd did just that, joining the Marine Corps Reserve and venturing off to boot camp in San Diego. I was amazed at the change in him sixteen weeks later. He was tall at six three, his uniform neatly pressed. He'd lost nearly twenty pounds and didn't have an ounce of fat on him. His short cropped hair lent him a serious look. He had a huge smile on his face as he returned our hugs. Other recruits were greeting their families when their drill sergeant interrupted our conversation with a growl. "Wipe those smiles off your faces!" The serious looks returned to their faces as the visitors quickly took their places in the auditorium for the graduation ceremony.

After advanced training, Todd moved back home, attended school, and graduated from the University of Washington with a double degree in Physics and Mathematics. The Marine Corps gave him the confidence and assurance that he could do his very best—and he did.

Those final two years Todd lived with us gave him and Bill a second chance to build a relationship—as friends this time. Bill often said, "I'm so glad I got another chance to be the dad I always wanted to be for Todd." They climbed mountains in the North Cascades, performed technical climbs at Smith Rock, hunted ducks and geese, and built Todd's airplane, the Hot To

Go. They were best friends until Bill died, talking on the phone nearly every day.

As a salute and honor to his dad, Todd arranged for the Hot To Go to be flown over Bill's graveside service as a final farewell. Bill would have thought it a high honor—and I believe he was cheering in heaven that day.

Todd flying formation with the Black Jacks in the Hot to Go.

CHAPTER 18

MOUNTAINS

"Everybody needs beauty as well as bread, places
to play in and pray in, where nature may heal
and give strength to body and soul alike."
—John Muir

"Did I tell you I'm climbing Mount St. Helens next month?" I asked Jim as we hiked Dog Mountain one hazy September day.

"You are?" Jim took a sip from his water bottle and tossed a handful of trail mix into his mouth. "I'd love to do that with you!"

Climbing permits were hard to come by, but Jim did some investigating and soon found one.

After training on several practice hikes, the big event arrived. I sighed as I looked at an October sky as blue as a robin's egg. The wind ruffled my hair and I glanced down at my dust-covered legs, smiling at Jim. I was tired. This was my eleventh climb up the historic peak.

I thought back to my first ascent on a hot August day in 1988. I had been excited to climb the ice-cream-cone-shaped mountain that stood at 8,366 feet after a volcanic eruption in May 1980.

Bill served as our capable leader and we were accompanied by climbers of various ages from eight to sixty-five. Our fifteen-year-old daughter Erika was also making the trek. All the climbers were anxious to get moving but they circled Bill, shuffling in their climbing clothes, clutching walking sticks, and adjusting backpacks. "No one goes in front of me or behind my assistant," he admonished. "Stay in the group and we'll have a good time." Throughout the day, Bill checked in with everyone. "Do you have any hot spots on your feet? Did you get a drink of water?" He made sure to provide a rest every hour, keeping up our stamina as we admired faraway views of Portland and other mountain peaks—Mount Hood, Mount Rainier, and Mount Adams. "Okay, guys. Time to get going!" Bill would say after ten minutes.

Erika, Bill, and I continued that long, hot, dusty trudge up the rock and sand. Most of the snow on the trail was gone but there were dirty piles of drifts farther away. It took eight hours to summit and the last part of the climb covered a loose, sandy slope. We would take one step only to slide down several feet. Then we'd try again and gain a few more feet. But the view at the top was worth the climb.

The crater was much larger than it looked from fifty miles away in our Vancouver home. We heard a droning in the distance and what looked like a tiny toy plane approached the center of the huge hole. We rested on the windy summit, putting our jackets on, devouring lunches of cheese and bagels while snapping photos of each other. The climb down was even harder than going up. My quads were tired and wobbly, my feet uncertain. Still, I continued the descent, glad we had completed the climb. We treated ourselves to pizza before starting the two-hour drive home.

Twenty-five years later with Jim, so much had changed. I was older—but the mountain had evolved, too. Its sandy slope merged among large chunks of massive rock. In the parking lot our leader said, "See you at the top!" and he turned and went on his way. No words of caution or instruction. Jim and I looked at each other. *This is really different from Bill,* I thought. But I comforted myself with the fact I was an experienced climber and in good physical shape. I could do this!

We trudged ahead through the nearly dark forest trail up a route called Monitor Ridge. It gradually became steeper and soon we needed to shed clothes despite the cool October morning. As we began to clear the trees, we gasped at the setting, shimmering full moon. *This is why I do this!* I thought.

We stopped at the last "real" restroom: a smelly, composting toilet in the woods. As we entered the timberline, I glanced up at a formidable pile of rocks. Large posts placed in strategic places marked the route. Rocks the size of refrigerators looked unfamiliar. We would take one step, hoist ourselves over a rock and then take another step. It was hard. Harder than the last time. I sighed again and looked back at Jim. "How are you doing, honey?"

Jim leaned wearily into the trail but gave me a quick grin when he heard my question. "Great. How much farther to the top?"

"Oh, quite a bit further." I wanted to be honest without discouraging him. I'd told him about false summits that trick you into thinking you're nearly there when you aren't.

We continued at a good pace, challenged by the huge rocks and refreshed by hourly breaks. As we munched trail mix and sipped Gatorade, I shared my hopes that we were going the right way. "Our climbing leader is so different than Bill." When I glanced around, I didn't see anyone nearby. We stood, put on our packs, and began climbing again. As we mantled—putting our arms on the rock above, drawing our legs and bodies up to the next set of rocks—I saw some climbers much farther to my right. Yikes! We *were* in the wrong spot! Afraid we might get into a precarious position, I told Jim we needed to head that way. Finally, closer to the others, I felt more at ease. We toiled up the rocks and sand. I sighed, wanting to quit, but I knew we needed to get to the top, if for no one but Jim.

As I moved slowly upward, I heard Jim muttering. I listened closely. "'You have searched me, Lord, and you know me. You know when I sit and when I rise; you perceive my thoughts from afar.'[12] It helps when I quote the Psalms when I'm having a hard run," he said. "I figure it will work for this, too."

"Thank you," I gasped. "It does."

"Oh, look," Jim said. "I see Andrew and Caleb over there." My two grandsons, age fourteen and twelve, were nearly jogging up the rocks. "There's Erika, too. Look at her go!"

She was in good shape; she had youth on her side and kept to a strict walking regimen that summer. I was proud of her. A mother and homeschool teacher to four kids, her name meant "strong" and indeed, the name fit well. It had been forty years, but I remembered her birth as though it was yesterday.

CHAPTER 19

ERIKA ANN

"A daughter is just a little girl who grows
up to be your best friend!"
—Joanne Fink, creator of Zenspirations

The nursery was complete, down to the taffeta which draped the old-fashioned, yellow wicker bassinet. Each of Mom Rudberg's babies had slept in that bassinet and we had continued the tradition with Todd, who was now five. I arranged the long skirt flowing from bassinet to floor—turquoise because we didn't know if the new baby would be a boy or girl. I painted the dresser peach with yellow daisies framing white drawer knobs. For the remainder of the nine months, I crossed my fingers. I loved my boy but wanted a girl.

I was determined I would stay home for this baby, as I hadn't been able to with Todd. We'd purchased our first little home in Vancouver where, as luck would have it, a neighboring street revealed a view of snowy Mount Hood outside our front window. Rhododendrons bloomed in the backyard all spring and Bill had cleared a garden for me to tend and harvest.

Monday, June 26 was a hot summer day. I cleaned the house, drove to the library to find books for my hospital stay, and rode bikes with Todd to a nearby store for milk. He pedaled double-time, working hard to keep up with me on his twenty-inch bike. Even at five years old, he was competitive and made every effort to keep up with his very awkward, pregnant mother. Those extra eight days after the due date had dragged on. Were the mild twinges of pressure on my belly early labor contractions?

"We're just checking to see if that baby is here yet!" Betsy said as she breezed into the house with her best friend. She'd brought ice cream bars for all of us.

After we finished the cool treats, the mild twinges turned into more earnest, painful pressure. At the hospital only two hours later, the baby arrived.

I was exhausted but giddy. "What is it?"

"It's a girl!"

My heart leaped with joy, but then I felt a pang of fear. The room was strangely quiet. There was no lusty newborn cry. The baby was the color of chalk.

In my dreamlike state, I watched as if from a distance, knowing the medical staff would take care of her. After all, this was the largest birthing center in Oregon.

Little did I know that my baby's life was hanging by a thread. After five minutes—a long time to be without oxygen—she began to breathe. And yet it may have been better that Erika did not breathe right away. Meconium had been present in the amniotic fluid, a substance dangerous to newborns if breathed into tender lungs.

The labor nurse quickly wrapped my baby in a warm blanket and alerted the doctor. They worked in one corner of the delivery room as I lay on the table. At last, I could hear low voices. "She's breathing now; let's get her up to the nursery." In those days they didn't have an ICU for newborns as they do now. They whisked her off where I could not see her for hours, unable to touch or nuzzle her, to nurse her, or examine her tiny fingers and toes.

Bill came into the recovery room. "Should I call the prayer chain at church?"

"Yes," I said feebly. I was beginning to come out of my high and wonder if our baby would be all right. Later in my room, a tech began to take blood samples.

For nearly twelve hours, there was no diagnosis for our baby. Finally, the pediatrician announced, "Your baby girl lost seventy-five percent of her blood during that precipitous delivery. Somehow it transfused back into your bloodstream. It's a good thing you have a different type of blood because it helped us discover the problem." Although in serious condition, the baby was a fighter. They administered a "super cell" blood transfusion and hoped for the best.

In the next three days, she improved. We named her Erika, choosing the Swedish spelling of the name to match her Swedish last name. Her middle name, Ann, was also my mother's. The first four days, my only connection with baby Erika was through the nursery window. I just wanted to hold her.

A woman wearing a hot pink volunteer jacket pushed a cart into my room. "Would you like to choose a book?"

"Oh, thank you, but I've brought some of my own." She turned away, wheeling the cart down the hall before I stopped her with my voice. "Wait a minute! Let me see what you have." I picked up a thick, paperback Bible. "I'll take this."

Although I'd been a Christian for many years and Bill and I were regular churchgoers, I usually opened my Bible only on Sundays. I was ashamed by the realization that I rarely called on God except in trouble. Was I was one of those Christians who used God just for "fire insurance" for eternity without taking the time to *know* Him? I was selfishly living my life on *my* own terms, expecting it to be smooth and surprised when it wasn't problem-free. Right now, I needed to get back in touch with God.

I opened the Bible to a favorite passage in Romans 8.

Who shall separate us from the love of Christ? Shall trouble, or hardship . . . For I am convinced that neither death nor life, nor angels nor demons, neither the present nor the future, nor any powers, neither height nor depth, nor anything else in all creation, will be able to separate us from the love of God that is in Christ *Jesus* our Lord.[13]

I felt peace. I knew Erika was in God's hands and whatever happened to her would not be a surprise to Him. God was very real to me again and I remembered that He had always been there. It was I who had moved away.

On that fourth evening after Erika's birth, the nurse came in briskly and said, "Are you ready to hold your baby girl?"

"Oh yes!" We walked to the nursery where I sat in the rocking chair, trembling with joy as she placed Erika in my arms. At first, she seemed to belong to *them,* not me. But a few moments later, I was filled with love and awe and knew she was mine. I opened her blanket and examined her little body. She made soft baby noises as I lifted her to my shoulder and patted her back. I kissed her and breathed in her sweet smell.

"Your baby seems to be stabilizing, though there may be brain damage from the lack of oxygen," the doctor said. "Time will tell." To me, she seemed fine except for the shaved portion on the left side of her head where she'd had the blood transfusion—the sign that there had been problems. She was our miracle baby.

On Saturday morning, Bill and Todd picked me up from the hospital. Our baby had to stay and I reluctantly left her under the nurses' care. Returning home, I walked into the empty nursery amidst all that peach and turquoise. *What would I have done if she hadn't survived?* Next morning, the hospital called and told us we could come and pick up baby Erika.

I began to read my Bible. All the scriptures seemed to open up and become real to me. No longer did I read out of duty, but because I *wanted* to.

Jim interrupted my thoughts, bringing me back to the hot, dusty mountain climb. "Erika is one strong woman. No wonder you're proud!" He paused a moment and asked, "Is there anything more you'd like me to know about her?"

In elementary school, I helped Erika study for tests. She worked diligently in school and I'd wait for news after we'd worked for hours the night before. One day she came home disheartened. "I got a D. What's wrong with me, Mom? Why can't I do better when I study so hard?" I cried with her and prayed, wanting answers in this struggle. Teachers told us, "Don't worry; she's just suffering from test anxiety." We knew it had to be more than that and finally, when Erika was a freshman in high school, we had a full psychological and physiological evaluation.

"Most children would have given up by this time," the psychologist told us. "Erika has a strong self-image, and she's tenacious. It's prevented her from giving up." I thought about the name we gave her, *Strong One*, which she reflected to her core. The assessment revealed damage to the memory portion of her brain and recommended therapy. A learning disability therapist worked with Erika for more than a year.

Eventually, Erika performed better in school. Even so, one of her high school advisors said, "You'll never go to college. You should try to get a vocation outside of higher education." But Erika was determined to prove the advisor wrong. She went on to college, majored in education, and became a certified teacher.

Her first teaching position was in kindergarten at Portland Christian School, where I also taught. The school was her alma mater so the opportunity was even more special. Erika's experience with her own learning disabilities made her compassionate toward students struggling in the classroom.

For three years, we taught together at Portland Christian School. She taught kindergarten and second grade, while I was the music teacher and librarian. I treasure those memories.

Many times Erika listened to my grief and sorrowed with me in the loss of her dad. Then Blair was gone, too. Once again, she was there, ready to hear me cry and comfort me. I can't imagine life without my daughter—she is also my best friend. I'm so grateful her life did not end in the delivery room those forty-some years ago.

CHAPTER 20

CLIMBING DOWN: JUST AS DIFFICULT AS GOING UP

"Climbing to the top is optional.
Getting down is mandatory!"
—Ed Viesturs

"Hey! You made it!" Andrew and Caleb shouted as Jim and I slowly made our way up the last slope to the summit. We high-fived each other, removed our packs, and sat down. I took a deep breath and looked around. The view on top was as I remembered it— all-encompassing—with a silence that screamed. You could hear the voices of the climbers but they were muted, as if the magnificence had pulled the sound from their voices.

We did the usual summit photos, ate, and drank. A breeze reminded us to zip up our jackets. Soon it was time to put on a fresh pair of socks, pick up our packs, and begin the descent.

Mount St. Helens Summit (Pictured L-R: Grandson Andrew,
Jim, Shirley, Daughter Erika, Grandson Caleb).

Going down, we were tired and the rocks appeared more enormous than ever. We took one slow step after another. About a third of the way back, we descended onto on a narrow ridge. Jim turned around, forgetting that his backpack added extra width to his body, and collided with the rock wall. He lost his balance, bumping me as he fell about six feet off the narrow path onto a large rock below.

I held my breath in terror.

Jim didn't move.

I peered around to see if there was anyone nearby.

"Are you all right?" I called fearfully.

He sat up, looking shaky and uncertain. I began to wonder why we had come on this climb. Why had I encouraged him so strongly to join?

Jim remained still a few more minutes, shook his head, and stood up gingerly. "I think I'm okay," he said at last, brushing the dust and pebbles from his hands. Later, he found a platter-sized bruise on his bum, an indication of how hard he'd hit the ground.

We took it slower as we climbed down. Finally, we made it to the tree line and a level pathway. The warm afternoon had turned into a cool fall evening. "You did it, honey!" I told Jim.

"Thank you for letting me come along," he said as we walked to the car. "I'm glad we made it—but I don't care if we never climb St. Helens again!"

"I think I'm done with it, too," I chuckled. "Eleven times is enough!" We dropped our backpacks by the car with a thud. "I was really scared back there," I added. "Up on the mountain when I saw you fall."

"I know. I was, too."

"Watching you, I had a crazy thought," I told him. "What if I lose someone else I love? I love you so much—I didn't want you to get hurt, or worse.…" I couldn't finish that thought—it was too dreadful.

He gave my hand a squeeze and said, "I was scared too. I love you so much and I wouldn't want you to go through another loss… But I'm fine; it's okay." He smiled.

We climbed into the van with a sigh and headed home under darkening skies.

CHAPTER 21

CARRIE LYNN

"She is just as real as a mom with living children. For she is still a mother. She is the bereaved mother."
—Lindsey Henke

As I told Jim about the births of my son and daughter, I realized that I needed to review another birth—one that brought much pain and sorrow but changed my life dramatically.

Late in 1976, I discovered I was pregnant. It was a surprise—but a delightful one. We changed the bedrooms, giving Todd the smaller one and combining Erika's room with the nursery.

The nightmare began on a hot June morning. The smell of blossoms was in the air and the windows were open to the warm breeze. In my thirty-fourth week of pregnancy, I noticed that my preborn baby, resting near my heart, was very quiet. Too quiet. Up until that time, the baby had been active and prone to hiccups.

I gave the baby's bottom a nudge. "Come on Carrie or Matthew, wake up." But there was no response.

After two days, I feared the worst. I called the advice nurse, who told me I should come to the hospital and get checked out. In the exam room, Bill and I watched as the nurse carefully place the enlarged stethoscope on my tummy—there were no infant monitors in 1977. The doctor came in and tried to listen many times. They sent me to ultrasound where I watched the little image on the screen, not knowing what it revealed.

"I'm sorry, Mrs. Rudberg," the doctor said solemnly. "The baby is dead." Bill and I sat stunned.

"In order for your psyche to get used to this," he droned, "we'll let you go home and wait for a few days. The labor will most likely take place on its own because the fetus is toxic to your system. We will call you after a few days if labor doesn't begin." What was he saying? My baby was *toxic*?

We left in silence. I stared out the window of our car, not seeing anything. When we got home, the children and my mother-in-law wanted to know what we found out.

"The baby's dead!" I blurted, bursting into tears.

"I'm so sorry, Shirley," Marian responded with a hug. We all sat, speechless. Erika looked quietly from face to face, too young to understand. Nine-year-old Todd said, "Can't we pray and ask God to heal it and bring it back to life?" I was ashamed that I didn't believe such a thing could happen. Why was my faith so weak? I didn't answer his question.

Bill wanted to hold me, but I needed to move—to pace. *It's gone,* I kept thinking. *It's gone. My baby is gone!* The tears would not stop.

"The kids are hungry. Should we get some dinner?" Bill's voice broke. "I don't like to see you so sad." He grabbed me and held me in his strong arms. I relaxed and put my head on his chest. We held each other, unable to comprehend the news.

"I guess we do need to eat," I said slowly.

"How about Skippers?" We drove to the casual seafood restaurant nearby, a family favorite. I wasn't hungry but eating seemed the thing to do.

My family still needed clothing cleaned and meals prepared. The next day I washed clothes and hung them on the line in the warm summer air. I was surprised how *normal* everyone acted. I needed to go to the grocery store for milk and essentials but I dreaded leaving the house for fear of bumping into anyone I knew. In a sense, I was protecting them from the bad news.

To add one more fear to the mix, I was dreading the impending labor—which would only produce a corpse and not a living, breathing little one who would make our hearts happy.

It was a waiting game. Three days later, my doctor instructed me to come to the hospital where labor would be induced. After two more days, when Pitocin didn't induce labor, they prepared to take the baby via Caesarian section. And then one more procedure was discussed. "It would be simple to complete a tubal ligation," the doctor said. "For your future birth control."

I looked down at my hands in fear. I didn't feel ready for that decision, but I didn't want to experience another loss like this. As with many institutionalized procedures, convenience for the hospital was the priority. There was no space for grieving parents to wait to make such a life-changing decision.

"I—I guess that would be okay," I said. To this day, I wish I'd faced my fears and refused.

In order to spare my feelings, the hospital placed me in the orthopedic ward, away from mothers and their newborns.

"Mrs. Rudberg?" A dark-haired, petite young woman approached my bed.

"Yes?"

"I don't want to upset you, but we need to know what to do with the body."

I glanced down at my much less rounded tummy, a physical reminder that my baby was gone. My mind whirled as I tried to answer her. I was emotionally drained and said the first thing that came to my mind. "You take care of it."

I stopped her when she bustled out of the room. "What was it?" I quavered.

"It was a female," she said matter-of-factly, continuing out the door. *"Female."* Not *"baby girl."*

"I'm glad we didn't set the crib up yet," I said when we walked in the door at home. "What do I *do* with all of these things?" I gestured to the box of brand new infant clothes from the recent baby shower. I broke into tears and Bill held me tightly.

The summer days dragged by. I tried to not be sad for my children's sake. Yet it seemed the sorrow would never end.

One morning, the phone rang. "Hi Shirley," said my friend, Beckie. We had been pregnant together until my loss. "Would you mind watching Corey and Ryan this afternoon?"

We had a trade-off babysitting arrangement. Erika and three-year-old Ryan loved to play with each other, but I hadn't yet watched baby Corey.

I didn't realize how difficult it would be. Corey was fussy so I held him close, shushing him and walking around the house with him in my arms. His sweet smell of baby powder and lotion reminded me that I would never hold my own little one. Never see her smile, never dry her tears, never hold her tight. My lips trembled as I held back the tears. My arms ached for my own child.

At the end of the summer, we put our house up for sale. Even so, we couldn't move away from the pain—it followed us.

Grief has a way of packing up her bags and moving in with you as an unwanted guest. Moving somewhere else only puts you in another place; the pain stays.

Bill, dealing with his own sadness, didn't know how to help other than hold me tight against his chest as I wept. Our grief drew us closer.

Finally, after a year of mourning, I said to Bill, "I'm tired of talking about 'the baby.' We need to give her a name."

"We planned on Carrie for a girl. What about a middle name?"

We talked for a time and decided on Carrie Lynn. That salved my hurt a little, though the wound was still there. *Maybe I'll always feel sad about Carrie,* I thought. I was haunted by the fact that she had no resting place, no marker to say she ever existed on earth.

I was comforted by the story of King David. When his infant son was very ill, David refused to eat or drink. When he was told the baby had died, he declared, "But now that he is dead, why should I fast? Could I bring the child back to life? I will some day go to where he is, but he can never come back to me."[14]

Scripture reveals the love Jesus Christ had for children. "Let the little children come to me, and do not hinder them, for the kingdom of God belongs to such as these."[15] My little Carrie was in heaven. Of that I was sure. I knew I'd see her some day. But when would this sadness end?

CHAPTER 22

CHANGE CAN HAPPEN AND IT DOES

"Just when I think I have learned the way to live, life changes!"
—Hugh Prather

Jim and I sat across the table from each other. The warmth of our shared dinner stood in sharp contrast to the sorrow I felt while telling my story.

"Wow. That was tough," Jim said, taking a sip of wine. "When Kara died at thirty-one, Kathy really never got over the loss." He shook his head at the memory. "It sounds like Bill was really there for you. When did your marriage get better?"

Should I be honest? I wondered. *Will he still want to be with me if I tell him the whole story?* I took a deep breath and continued.

Bill and I were "comfortable" with the norm even though we weren't happy. We developed a pattern of arguments, silent treatments, and making up. We argued about the normal things couples struggle with: parenting, finances, and sex.

We tried to make happy family memories, fishing and water-skiing in our new boat, visiting relatives, and exploring National Parks. Yet our marriage was growing tumultuous. We were two stubborn people wanting our own way.

"Look," Bill said one evening after another fight. "I can't take this anymore. Do you think a counselor might be able to help us?"

In my naïveté, I thought we'd go to the counselor's office to calmly and clearly tell our side of things. The counselor would explain what needed to happen and we would go home to make those changes.

This was a far cry from what we were about to do: take a long hard look at ourselves.

We saw a series of counselors. One helped us identify our dysfunctional marriage as like a patient. Bill and I were doctors tasked with diagnosing the problem, determining the cure, and healing the marriage. "How do you want your history to read?" another counselor challenged.

One morning in Sunday School, the teacher gave a routine call for prayer requests. Members usually brought up needs for healing or employment.

To my surprise, Bill raised his hand. "Shirley and I are having difficulties in our marriage and we're going to counseling," he said. "I'd like prayer for us to work out our problems." I looked down at my lap in embarrassment, pretending to read my notes. I was afraid our fellow church members would think less of us. Marriage problems were never discussed openly in our group. Would our friends judge us as weak Christians?

At the same time, I felt relief. That open, honest request and the willingness to acknowledge that we needed help began to turn things around.

In order to change things, we needed to talk about our problems. This was tough for me, as I would often clam up in fear of angering Bill. The counselor recommended a communication class for couples through Kaiser Permanente. I was hopeful but secretly afraid it wouldn't work. But we enrolled in the class and that's when things really started to change.

Weekly, we were given tools to communicate. We read books and discussed them. We learned to listen carefully during conflict without interrupting. When the other person finished talking, instead of being defensive, we listened and repeated back what we heard. If we didn't hear it correctly, it was said again. We learned to be more honest—even if it hurt—while communicating our feelings in a respectful way. The honesty was freeing.

Bill's anger could make it hard for him to communicate. He learned to say, "I'm angry right now. Please let me sort this out. Then we can set a time to talk."

Early in my marriage, I had read a lot of books that told me *I* was the one who needed to change. They advised me to "give in," "let him have his way," or "submit." True: I needed to change. But changing how I interacted with Bill made the most powerful difference.

I read, "For the Spirit God gave us does not make us timid, but gives us power, love and self-discipline."[16] I asked the Holy Spirit to give me the strength to not fear Bill's reactions.

One afternoon, Bill came in the door with a frown on his face. "Hi honey," I said, trying to sound cheerful. I attempted to greet him with a hug and kiss but he stomped past and pushed me away.

"Just leave me alone," he growled.

Instead of responding as usual and thinking I'd done something to offend him, I decided to confront his anger. *What's the worst thing that can happen?* I took a deep breath and said in a calm voice—instead of sarcastic or angry—"Look, I'm not sure what's going on here, but I'm not going to take on your anger. You might have good reason to feel this way, but I know it isn't me." I left the room and started dinner.

A while later he stepped into the kitchen. "I'm not upset with you. It's something that happened at work. I'm really ticked—I'm going for a hike." He closed the door behind him, no longer as angry as he had been minutes earlier. My challenge to him had helped both of us. Though I had wanted to "fix" his feelings, I learned to give him space to work them out himself.

I also began to do little things I knew Bill would appreciate. One morning, I found a note from him. *Thank you for cleaning out my bathroom drawer. It was a nice surprise to see everything organized.* The note made my day—over what had been a simple, two-minute task.

Two words we learned to avoid were "always" and "never." We began using the phrase, "I feel" to replace "you made me feel." We took ownership for our feelings. We also learned that some things weren't worth arguing about.

For years, Bill had done his thing and I had done mine. Now we purposed to have "planned pleasant activities," setting a date at least once a week to walk, go out for dinner, or get a cup of coffee together.

We took a mountaineering class, enjoying each step of the journey as we trained, shopped for gear, and made our graduation climb. It was something I'd never dreamed of doing and I *liked* it! I pushed back my fear of heights and edges to ascend the steep-edged trail. After that, we backpacked, rock climbed, and continued mountaineering. Our kids joined us for some adventures but many we did alone. Our relationship gradually transformed.

"What was the hardest climb you ever did?" Jim asked as I relayed the story. We had finished dinner and began to clear the table. I paused a moment to grind decaf coffee beans and continued our climb story.

The first time Bill and I climbed Mount Hood, the weather changed as we summited and we faced a near whiteout. It was hard to know we were even at the top. My backpack straps weren't padded and my shoulders were tense and sore. By the time we got to the "hogsback"—the ridge near the summit of Mount Hood—I was in tears because of the pain. While we roped up, Bill removed my pack and set it by a rock. "We'll pick this up on our way down," he said. We continued our trudge up the snowy ridge, following our leader, Larry.

After we climbed the "chute" roped up to Larry, he announced, "Congratulations, you're at the top. Now turn around, we're going back down!" After finishing the climb in the agonizing cold, we celebrated at the Huckleberry Inn in Government Camp, heady with the wonderful experience of working hard and completing a task together. We did it!

We climbed Hood together five more times and also ascended Mount Adams, the second-tallest mountain in Washington. We took long, steep hikes through waterfalls and steep, green-treed trails in the Columbia River Gorge, learning to carry weighty packs. We climbed a majority of the volcanic peaks in Oregon: Eagle Cap, Mount Thielsen, Mount Washington, Mount Bailey, Broken Top, South Sister, Mount Bachelor, and Three-Fingered Jack—all challenging climbs.

One hot summer afternoon on Mount Thielsen, we were climbing over large flat rocks and broken rock fragments several feet deep along the slope of the mountain. It was a challenge to keep our balance while ascending the rock-laden route. We took three steps forward, then two steps back.

The night before, we had unsuccessfully attempted to sleep in our car and we were tired. Bill's dinner hadn't agreed with him. The hot sun felt like a furnace. Two hundred feet from the summit, Bill looked up, squinted in the bright sun and said, "Let's turn around. I'm done."

"Whatever you say," I said, surprised that—for the first time—he wasn't finishing a climb.

Glad to be done for the weekend, I learned that it's all right to give in to fatigue—especially on a dangerous journey. Bill was a wise leader who took precautions and made good decisions. Neither of us ever got hurt.

Each mountain climb had its own story. Mount Washington had a seven-thousand-foot drop-off; Broken Top had beautiful, black, shiny obsidian; South Sister was full of mosquitoes that bit through our clothing. What was important about these climbs is that we did them together. All the experiences made us stronger and drew us closer.

Over the next twenty years, we never went back to our old ways of handling our disagreements. Our children also appreciated the changes in us. In nearly every anniversary card they sent us, they thanked us for staying together.

CHAPTER 23

STICKING THROUGH THE TOUGH TIMES

"Safe in the Arms of Jesus."
—Fanny J. Crosby, 1868

Our children grew up, married, and moved away. Now there were six grandchildren. Bill and I continued our adventures together. And then on February 3, 2006, Bill met his baby girl, Carrie Lynn, in heaven.

I never could have imagined how much I'd miss his companionship and love. My bed seemed yawningly huge without him. I traded my side of the bed and slept in his spot. It helped somehow.

Four months after Bill died, I was forced to find a new job. After searching for teaching positions, I found a job in a completely different field at Columbia Machine, the manufacturing company where Bill worked for thirty-five years.

My new position was as a planner in the Production Control Department. I walked in the departments where Bill walked and came across his work on prints and drawings. It helped me realize he was gone and work through the grief.

After two years, I yearned for another soulmate. A bright light came into my life and changed it forever when I met Blair in 2008. We married six months later. I changed jobs again, becoming a part-time music teacher in the same school district where Blair taught. Our families blended wonderfully.

Blair taught me pure love and trust. Our adjustment to marriage was as close as possible to heaven on earth. It seemed we'd have many years together. We traveled to meet and visit with family, enjoying winters and summers in Colorado, California, Arizona, Hawaii, and Pennsylvania. In mid-November, we journeyed to South Africa for six weeks where we met the family of Blair's late wife. We rented a car and drove from Johannesburg to Cape Town in the beautiful, varied country. It was an experience of a lifetime.

One month after that memorable trip, tragedy struck. Blair felt faint one evening and complained of pain in his head. As we waited for the ambulance, I knelt by his side and prayed for the paramedics to help. Moments after I prayed and recited Psalm 23, Blair lost consciousness. He died the next day.

It was impossible not question God in my grief as I faced widowhood for a second time. I paced the halls and stairs of my house. I read books. The Bible was the most comforting; it gave me solace. I rearranged my home and upstairs photo gallery, my heart breaking as I reviewed trip photos with Blair. I asked for God's comfort on sleepless nights, dining alone, traveling alone, and sitting in church by myself. I learned again that God is fully trustworthy.

Ultimately, I chose to be grateful for what Blair and I had. Instead of becoming bitter, I depended on my Heavenly Father to take care of me and use me right where I was. The two years of receiving Blair's love had made my life richer.

A suggestion in one of the books on grief[17] helped me make a giant step forward. The idea was to make a list of all the people in my life who had died. I examined each name on the list, reflecting whether or not I had truly grieved. I discovered that I had done the work of grief in every case except one: the baby girl we named Carrie Lynn.

I wrote Carrie a letter. I told her I was sorry I'd never gotten to see, touch, or hold her. I regretted not having a proper burial. I faced the fact I didn't know what they did with her body—and I acknowledged my guilt for not knowing. I confessed to God that I had overreacted in my hurt. He forgave me. Now I needed to forgive myself.

Five months after Blair died, even though I didn't know where her body was, I ordered a stone with her name on it.

Carrie Lynn Rudberg
Stillborn
June 13, 1977
"Safe in the arms of Jesus"

The marker held an image of Jesus holding a baby in His arms. I had it placed near her father's headstone and arranged a graveside service to bring closure to my grief journey.

Dear Carrie,

I am so glad this marker is finally here to say you lived a life—though it was short. The minute your life ended you were in God's presence. I'm so grateful that life on earth is not the end but the beginning of an eternity which never ends.

I look forward to looking into your eyes, taking your hand, and exploring heaven with you.

Goodbye, little Carrie Lynn. I love you!

At Carrie's headstone.

CHAPTER 24

WILL YOU MARRY ME?

*"Marriage is not a noun; it's a verb. It isn't something
you get. It's something you do. Every day!"*
—Barbara De Angelis

"Have you ever been to the Grotto?" Jim asked as we drove across the I-205 bridge on our way to Ashland.

"No, I haven't," I admitted, although I'd heard about the sixty-two-acre Catholic shrine and botanical garden in northeast Portland. "I'd love to see it."

The sun was hidden behind clouds and the morning was cool. We strolled along a quiet pathway in the dim light. Green ferns flourished in the rocky gardens. The high-windowed clerestory looked mysterious in the soft light. As we strolled along, hand in hand, Jim told me he liked to come here and pray. Soon a larger-than-life statue of Jesus carrying the cross loomed into view. "Oh, that's beautiful!" I breathed as I looked up.

"This is called the Christus Statue. Let's stop here for a moment." Jim paused. "Turn this way, so I can see your face while also looking at the face of Jesus."

I turned as he asked and he knelt, facing me. My heart quickened as I began to realize what Jim's intentions were. *What will I say?*

"I just want to say this in front of this statue of Jesus, the One who guides me in everything I do." He took my hand. "Shirley Quiring Rudberg Graybill, will you marry me?" In his left hand, he held a small box.

I drew a quick breath. *Did I really hear what I think I heard?*

"Yes!" I said, as certainty flooded my mind. "I will!" Jim picked me up in his arms and swung me around with joy. I giggled shyly, filled with tummy-pinging delight. My body was suffused with joy and relief that I had met such a quality guy. Someone absolutely perfect for me!

Nestled in the jeweler's box was a carat diamond flanked by two rubies and sprinkled with tiny diamonds in a white-gold setting. It was even more beautiful on my left ring finger.

"Do you like the ring?" Jim asked. "I thought the rubies fit so well since you like red."

"I *love* it!" I enthused.

The gray skies were turning blue. The sun peeked out and soon it was bright and sunny. As we slowly left the garden, holding hands, I turned and looked back once more at the statue of Jesus. Jim put his arm around me and pulled me into an embrace.

"Would you mind if we prayed together?"

"Of course not." My heart soared with joy that this was important to him.

We're engaged!

After asking God to bless our newly committed relationship. Jim concluded with a ringing voice, "In Your precious name, Amen."

In the car we exchanged a long, sweet kiss. Jim reached in the backseat. "A little something I got for you."

"But you've already given me something!" I exclaimed. Inside the package was a brown leather book, *Jesus Calling* by Sarah Young. Both of us had used the book as part of our separate, daily devotions. The leather bound book had an inscription on the front. *To my Shirley, Your Jim always.* "I love it!" I said as I paged through the expanded edition.

"I thought we could use this one for devotions together, after we get married," Jim said. I kissed him again, grateful that devotions were a priority.

"Well," Jim said matter-of-factly, "let's get going. We have lots of miles to cover!" and we continued on our way to Ashland.

"When should we get married?" I asked.

"The sooner the better, *I* think!" he joked. "Christmas is my favorite time of the year. I think we should have a Christmas wedding!"

We could fit at least a week's honeymoon into December before the busyness of Christmas took place. Could we be ready for a wedding in three months?

"What do you think your kids will say?" I asked.

"They'll support me but will think I'm a little crazy, too." Jim chuckled, shook his head, and turned to me with a smile. "I was engaged to LaRay only a year after Kathy died. People warned me I was moving too quickly—not fully grieving Kathy's death. But I thought I could make it work. From my past relationships, I learned not to give up. Yet even my pastor counseled me to slow down."

"What finally made you break the engagement?" I quizzed.

"We talked about ourselves for an entire hour-long counseling session, and the counselor said, 'Jim, you're an Italian racehorse—a mover and shaker. LaRay is not. You've overwhelmed her and will continue to do so. I don't think the two of you are going to work.'

"We left the office, shaken, and soon decided to go our separate ways. I'm so glad it didn't work, for I wouldn't have met you!"

"That reminds me of my experience with Ron. He wasn't right for me either. I think we both wanted to recreate something that can't happen until the time is right."

Long drives are good for confidential talks, so by the time we arrived in Ashland, we had become even more close. I felt I'd known Jim all my life.

After enjoying *My Fair Lady* and a night's sleep in our rooms, Jim picked me up for breakfast. The sun warmed our backs as we sipped lattes and ate savory pastries in an outdoor cafe.

"Let's take a drive up to Mount Ashland," Jim suggested. We walked among boulders on the dusty summit and marveled at the expanded vista of the valley below. It was hot so we took a break in the air-conditioned car to listen to CDs. It was not music we listened to but the memorial services of our beloved mates: Bill (February 3, 2006), Blair (January 31, 2010), and Kathy (July 25, 2011).

As we listened, crying and holding each other tightly, we understood the tears in a way many others could not. I learned that Kathy had been a woman of quality who had shared a life of love with Jim—as had I.

Driving back to Vancouver on Sunday afternoon, we talked about sorting our accumulated possessions and finding a home that would be *ours*. "I'll need to call Erika tonight," I thought aloud. "I want to tell her myself that we're engaged."

I remembered with chagrin when Ron and I had made the engagement announcement. I'd invited Erika and the family for brunch where they met him for the first time. Both Erika and Trent were dumbfounded at the news. Erika had called me later. "What are you doing, Mom? You hardly know this man!"

"He's a good man. Don't worry."

"I *do* worry. You are rushing this marriage."

She was right, of course. I had felt out of whack during that entire engagement.

When Jim dropped me off at Erika and Trent's, I told them my exciting news in a rush. This time there were smiles and hugs all around.

"Why do you feel differently about Jim?" I asked, relieved and curious.

"I feel he is more right for you," Erika explained. "When we met him at the church picnic, I thought, 'This guy is the one!' It looks like I was right!"

Jim joined us later that evening, greeted with pleasure by Erika's family. We chatted excitedly about our plans.

"Do you know I love your Grammie very much?" he said playfully to Annabel and Emily, who shrugged and giggled at each other.

CHAPTER 25

BINDING FAMILY TIES

"Families are like fudge . . . mostly sweet with a few nuts."
—Unknown

Jim had three married children, two stepchildren, and nine grandchildren. I had two children, two stepsons, and seven grandchildren. Not to mention extended family—siblings, in-laws, nieces, nephews, great-nieces, and great-nephews. Jim's mother and stepfather were still alive, as were my in-laws from both marriages, including Bill's ninety-two-year-old mother. We were overwhelmed with family.

I reflected on our family connections as I prepared for a talk at a church women's group. In that moment, I realized a special thread of hope that tied our three generations together.

It was soon after the loss of Carrie and we were celebrating Erika's fourth birthday. As we were driving to pick up some items for her birthday party, Erika asked, "Mommy, where's the baby?"

"Sweetheart, she died and now she's in heaven with Jesus."

"Will I see her?"

"Yes. Everyone who invites Jesus into their hearts will go to heaven. The baby is there."

"Did the baby ask Jesus into her heart?" she asked, cocking her head.

"No. She couldn't talk yet. But the Bible shows how much Jesus loves children and He wants them to be with Him." I reminded her of the story about Jesus blessing the children. "She didn't have a chance to ask Jesus into her heart because she was so little, but I know she's in heaven. God loves her very, very much. Just like He loves you, sweetie."

"I want to see the baby." She hesitated. "And Jesus."

"Would you like to ask Him into your heart?"

"Yes." She bowed her little blonde head, squeezing her eyes tightly. "Dear Jesus," she said in her husky voice. "I want you to come in to my heart. Amen." She nodded affirmatively and said the last word with emphasis.

"Jesus wants us to obey Him and our parents on earth," I said gently. "When He comes into your heart, you need to obey Him and be obedient to your mommy and daddy."

"I *want* to be a good girl."

"I know you do. And you can ask Jesus to help you do that, too."

She bowed her head again. "And Jesus, please help me be good and not pester my brother . . . and to obey mommy and daddy."

When I shared this with Jim, he exclaimed, "Didn't you say that you were four when you accepted Jesus? You were in a cemetery with your brother and looking at your friend's grave."

"Yes, that's part of what I realized! But there's more."

When I was planning Blair's funeral, Erika stopped by with four-year-old Emily.

"Where's Grandpa Blair?" Emily piped up.

"Grandpa Blair went to heaven," Erika answered in a soft voice. Emily looked at us, puzzled and unable to piece together that her Grandpa Blair had died and gone to heaven only two days before.

As they drove home together, Erika said, "Dying means you don't live here anymore. Everybody dies sometime. And if Jesus is in your heart," she explained, "you'll be with Him in heaven after you die."

"I want to ask Jesus in my heart!" said Emily. Erika reached over, squeezed her hand, and they prayed.

The angels were rejoicing for "Emilee," as Blair called her. He was rejoicing too.

"It was death that moved three little girls to invite Jesus Christ into their lives," said Jim, shaking his head with emotion. "That's an amazing story . . ."

As the old hymn says, "God moves in a mysterious way; His wonders to perform."

And we knew there would be more wonders—perhaps less momentous, but still joyous—as we shared our lives with all our host of family.

Three generations: Erika, Emily, Shirley.

CHAPTER 26

WE'RE GETTING MARRIED!

"May the God of hope fill you with all joy and
peace as you trust in Him, so that you may overflow
with hope by the power of the Holy Spirit."
—Romans 15:13

We found the perfect home near the Columbia River. As we talked and planned our move, we learned even more about each other. What should we keep and what should we give away?

Should I keep the beautiful red couch with the cream dragonfly pattern that Blair and I had shared? It held so many memories. Blair and I, watching movies together. Me by the fire, lonely and grieving. And then with Jim, holding hands. Finally, I decided to make the couch a focal point in our new great room.

Combined, we had accumulated nearly eighty years of possessions. We gave much away to family and charity. We then went to work on the house—painting walls, removing old carpets and floors, adding golden oak hardwood to the main rooms and tile to our bath. A landscaper transformed the backyard into a sanctuary with a view of the river. After a furious twelve weeks, the house was ready.

We planned to settle in our new home a little at a time, getting the kitchen in order before the wedding. Each morning, Jim and I would have coffee together and plan the day. Our tasks might include shopping for light fixtures, signing loan papers, arranging wedding details, or applying for our marriage license. I found that even though we were having a simple wedding, it required as much planning as a larger affair.

Saturday morning: moving day. I wrote in my journal:

Two weeks from tomorrow, I will take vows to Jim.

I said those vows when I was nineteen. Though I knew they were serious, I had no idea what they really meant. I just wanted to get married!

I said them again to Blair forty-two years later. I understood better how serious the vows were. It was easy to say "to love and to cherish, in sickness and in health." When I said "till death us do part" my voice broke as I was filled with memories of the choking loss of Bill two years earlier. Yet it was with hope I said them.

In two weeks, I may falter with those words but I will say them with hope. For God has gifted me with a wonderful man who loves and cherishes me. I will say, "For better, for worse, for richer, for poorer, in sickness or in health, to love and to cherish till death do us part."

Finally the week of our wedding arrived. It was cold—in the low twenties. On Friday it snowed an inch. I worried about the weather preventing people from coming to the ceremony.

Friday evening, my sister hosted an intimate gathering. She and Connie served appetizers with champagne and sparkling cider while Jim and I reveled in the company of our family and close friends.

Jim and I were the first to leave that evening. We knew we needed a full night's sleep. On a makeshift air mattress, I slept in my house for the very last time. I had lived there five years, creating memories both joyous and sad. Now I looked forward to a new life and more history.

CHAPTER 27

WEDDING DAY

"I, Shirley, take you, Jim, to be my wedded husband . . ."

Saturday, December 7 dawned cold and clear. I drove into the church parking lot in the early morning light. The ground was sprinkled with snow like powdered sugar; the temperature hovered in the low teens. There was no wind; it was a still, cold day. My feet crunched snow as I walked quickly into the church from the parking lot.

I put on my dress: a red-laced sheath with a V-neck. The moment I had seen it, I'd known it was the one for me.

"Shirley, you look beautiful!" exclaimed my hairdresser. "You have such a cute figure!"

I felt great.

I knew Bill, my first love, had been the right man for me—in spite of marrying him at a mere nineteen. I had learned so much from him. He taught me persistence.

Marrying Blair had been right, too. Blair gave me love when I didn't think I'd ever experience it again. He showed me that a person doesn't need to be rigid to remain firm in belief.

God was so full of surprises. Incredibly, I asked God to bring someone into my life who loved Him more than anyone—and I also asked that he be crazy about me. And He did—He brought me Jim.

Wreaths with white lights twinkled on the walls. Two twenty-foot trees stood in the front corners of the sanctuary, infusing the air with holiday excitement. Sparkly stars and red poinsettias added to the festivity. Near the altar, a simple crèche held baby Jesus.

We had a brief rehearsal before guests began to arrive. Our photographer busily snapped pictures. I hoped she'd know who was who—there were so many in this new, blended family. Jim and I wanted to rehearse once more the song we'd sing together in the ceremony, but there wasn't time. "Unchained Melody" drifted from the piano before the soloist rehearsed "You Lift Me Up" once more.

The candles were lit; the music was playing. The oldest four granddaughters walked in: Rebekah, Taylor, Kennedy, and Sarah. The flower girls, Haley and Annabel, were next. Then Cole, carrying a pine box with two rings nestled inside. The youngest two, Emily and Rowan, had serious looks on their faces as they followed. The strains of "Canon in D" began, our cue to enter.

The day was perfect even though everything hadn't gone as planned. My son's two daughters had driven down from Seattle. When they came into the bride's room to freshen up, I asked, "Is your daddy here?"

"No. But he's on his way," they said. I felt a knot of concern but tried to brush it aside.

I also wondered about the family members I hadn't seen the night before. I had hoped everyone could have met that Friday evening. Yet each person had their own life and complications. My stepson Jonathan met Jim just minutes before the ceremony. There just wasn't enough time for all the conversations and introductions that I longed for.

Todd appeared at the sanctuary in the nick of time. I breathed a sigh of relief. True to form, he had flown his own airplane down from Seattle, taking this opportunity for adventure.

I glanced at a few faces. There was my daughter, biting her lip with tears in her eyes. My sister and brother brushed away tears of joy. And there on the other side of the sanctuary were grateful faces of joy for Jim, their brother and friend. Jim's mentally handicapped sister, Mary, laughed out loud with glee. It put a smile on everyone's face.

I took a deep breath as the wedding coordinator opened the doors. "Go ahead. It's time." Instead of being escorted down the center aisle, I walked in through a side door by myself. I tried to walk slowly but it was impossible.

Jim had a huge grin on his face as he walked quickly to meet me. He looked so handsome in his black tuxedo, white shirt, and red vest. His face was full of joy.

Pastor Paul Jackson opened the ceremony. "These two really, *really* want to get married!" And we did.

After the ceremony, we were toasted with touching words of congratulations from friends and family on both sides. I tossed my bouquet and unmarried women both young and old stood ready to see who would be married next. My friend Sue caught it. Our guests showered us with bubbles as we left the church. In the parking lot, our granddaughters opened a basket containing ten love birds. Jim and I were each given a dove and we released them into the icy blue sky to symbolize our love and commitment.

Then we hopped into Jim's car, off to change clothes and dash to the airport.

Jim and Shirley's blended family, minus seven (Picture L-R: Bryan, Austyn, Kennedy, Vicki, Caleb, Andrew, Rebekah, Todd, Sarah, Greg, Annabel, Shirley, Rowan, Jim, Jonathan, Emily, Trent, William, Erika, Aaron, Alexander, Cole, Taylor, Haley, Kryston, Kerri, Kevin. Missing: Tucker, Catherine, Meghan, Ryan, Jennifer, Landon, and Olivia).

CHAPTER 28

HONEYMOON: WHISTLER, CANADA

"Our body produces love chemicals which sustain the
honeymoon for about eighteen months. Then the honeymoon
ends . . ." and we get to begin to 'choose love'!"
—Shane & Phyllis Womack

We left the church in a wave of goodbyes, looked at each other, and said, "We did it!" We were exhausted. It had been an emotional, busy day—not including the weeks of preparation.

Jim parked the car in our driveway, the garage too full of boxes and extra furnishings. As he unlocked the front door, I wondered, *It's really true; we are married! Why has God so abundantly blessed me?*

"Get ready!" Jim said. He swooped me up, carried me through the entry, and set me down inside our new home. We wrapped our arms around each other and kissed again.

I dashed into the bedroom to change into jeans and shiny, black knee-high boots trimmed in gold buckles. Soon Jim's son and grandson, Bryan and Austyn, arrived. We piled our luggage into his car and headed to the airport.

It had long been dark when we arrived in Vancouver, B.C. We picked up our rental car and made our way north to Whistler. By the time we got to the ski town—known for hosting the winter Olympics a few years earlier—it was one thirty. We'd been up for twenty-three hours.

Jim and Shirley at the 2010 Winter Olympic Rings in Whistler, B.C.

We drove around the block several times, searching the dark, deserted streets for the parking garage to our suite. At last we noticed a car emerging from a garage below street level. Jim turned into the garage while the gate was open. As the gate lowered and locked behind us, we discovered we were in the wrong building. We waited for what seemed like an hour until another car came in and we could make our escape out the open gate. Eventually, we found the right building and garage. We collapsed into the bed, exhausted, and promptly fell asleep.

The condo was lovely, with a fireplace and a beautiful view of the snowy forest across the way. That first morning I opened my eyes to the morning sunlight and heard Jim's voice. "Here's some coffee for you, my love." This first cup began a tradition. Every morning, he brings a mug of fresh coffee, made just as I like it.

We were so happy to give our love to each other at last. Later we found breakfast in the nearby village. I was ravenous and so was

Jim. After our meal, we slowly walked back to our condo, holding mittened hands.

That evening we participated in "A Taste of Whistler," a guided restaurant tour with several other couples. As we ate each course, the chef described how our food had been prepared and seasoned. At the dessert stop, we drank ice wine. It was too sweet for our taste but we were glad we'd tried it once.

Next day, we explored the upper village and shopped in the tiny stores. We boarded the tram between two peaks, Black Comb and Whistler, glimpsing deep valleys and huge, snowy mountains thousands of feet below the floor window of our tram.

We took snowshoeing lessons one day. Another day, we rode the longest zip-line in North America. This reminded me of rappelling—of taking the first, scary step into nothingness. I went first on the zip-line, Jim standing beside me on the platform to remind me that I was securely attached and wouldn't fall. Once I stepped off, I began to enjoy the scenery.

In all of our interactions at the zip-line, in the tram, or at a restaurant, Jim would excitedly tell people, "We just got married! We never thought it would happen but we found love once again." The surprise and joy on people's faces reflected our own.

The week flew and soon it was time to return to reality. Arriving at home we were greeted by a welcome banner from Erika's family with hand-drawn pictures and messages. In less than two weeks, it would be Christmas. We chose a ten-foot tree to fill with hundreds of twinkly lights without any other decoration. It became another new tradition.

We cleared out boxes and removed clutter. Each day, we worked in one room before moving to the next. We did the "kid's room" first so it would be ready for an overnight visit from our grandkids. Soon we were even able to park the cars in the garage. We were a good team.

CHAPTER 29

THE FIRST HUNDRED DAYS AND BEYOND

"Weeping may endure for a night, but
joy cometh in the morning."
—Psalm 30:5 (KJV)

What can I say about the delight of waking up to a husband, lover, and partner? Waking up *with* someone instead of waking up alone—it was an indescribable sensation.

It's true: some days I enjoyed solitude. In my earlier life, I longed for it. But in the past eight years with a two-year respite in between, I'd found solitude highly overrated. I *liked* being married.

Jim would get up first. He'd turn on lamps, light candles, and start a fire to take the early morning chill out of the room. He would make coffee, the pot chiming when ready. "How's the coffee?" Jim would ask. Making my cup perfect was his goal.

Ahhh. The dark, French-roasted coffee with bubbles forming on the sides of the cup was always delightful. "So tasty!" I'd say.

We sat and enjoyed the fire. We talked quietly. Soon we'd get our Bibles and begin our daily reading. Jim would say a quick prayer. "Heavenly Father, show us what You want us to learn this day as we read Your Word." We recorded insights and prayer requests. Each day we prayed for a different segment of our family: our combined eight children, grandchildren, siblings. Jim's one day, mine the next; each day a different side of the family.

The first one hundred days of marriage. What can I say about them? Passion. Love. Late night talks when we never ran out of words.

We talked all morning, looking at the clock in surprise to discover it was nearly lunchtime and we were still in our pajamas. We experienced adventure, companionship, and long walks.

There was laughter, surprise, and joy as we compared likes and dislikes. How could he not appreciate jazz? We shared tasks: he dragged the central vacuum while I dusted.

Did I say love? It must be said again.

Our wedding vows were declarations we promised to keep.

> For better for worse,
> For richer for poorer,
> In sickness and in health,
> To love, cherish, and to obey,
> Till death us do part.

We were challenged with the "in sickness and in health" vow nine months after we married. One morning, a few days before we were to leave on an extended trip to Washington, D.C. and New York City, I stepped out of bed and noticed pain in my left foot. I could barely put weight on it. We made an appointment with Jim's brother, a podiatrist in Portland. John quickly assessed plantar fasciitis—an inflammation of the plantar ligament on the bottom of the foot. "Save your walking for the museums," he said. "By the way, do those bunions give you much trouble?"

"Well, the right one hurts pretty badly," I said.

"We can talk about surgery," John suggested. "After your plantar gets better."

Jim and I enjoyed New York City and Washington, D.C. The plantar fasciitis pain was ornery at times, but we made it through.

In January, I went ahead with surgery on the opposite foot. I was laid up for a week, propping up my cast hour by hour. I had envisioned loads of reading time and a chance to catch up on movies and TV programs. Instead, I was bored to tears! I was allowed a five-minute break, barely enough time to thump-step to the bathroom.

"How about I make those stuffed green peppers we talked about?" Jim asked.

"Sure," I said, heading to the bookshelf. I grabbed a thin, well-used volume with duct tape on the spine. It was my first ever cookbook, *Betty Crocker's Cookbook for Two.* "I usually substitute oatmeal for the bread crumbs," I said. "I use dehydrated onions—then there isn't as much moisture in the stuffing." Jim nodded as he busily gathered ingredients.

"Keep in mind, the recipe is only for half a pound of ground beef. Don't forget to cook the green peppers in boiling water for four minutes." I was starting to sound less friendly and more irritated.

"Thank you, honey." I could hear the meat sizzling as I wandered back into the kitchen. "Shouldn't you be off your feet?" he asked.

"What are you doing?" I asked, watching him at the counter. "Why are you doing that? You're not supposed to cook the meat now. It goes into the peppers raw!" My bossy teacher persona had taken over.

"I've cooked this before," he said mildly. "I just thought I'd do it this way." There was an edge to his voice.

"Okay . . . " I wandered back to the couch, uneasy. *Wish I could do this myself,* I thought.

"Would you mind if I used quinoa instead of oatmeal?" he asked, pouring hot water into a saucepan and adding the small grains.

"I guess not." But I wished he'd just follow the recipe. I made every attempt to stay seated on the couch rather than snoop at my husband's excellent attempts to put together dinner.

I thump-stepped into the kitchen with my cast. "What are you doing now?"

Jim turned and looked at me with a frown.

"I'm sorry. I don't want to be bossy. I—I just like it *my* way!" As I said it, I realized my words weren't an apology at all.

"How about you sit back down over there and I'll bring you a glass of wine before dinner?" He gently helped me back to the sofa.

Later, we ate the stuffed green peppers. I didn't think they were as tasty as usual—not my well-loved comfort food. Jim didn't think they were spicy enough.

With diplomacy and love in his voice, Jim said, "Next time, honey, why don't I just follow your recipe? You are the expert, having done this more than I have."

Feeling guilty, I said, "I'll try to stay out of your way when you cook. You've been doing a wonderful job."

And so we resolved what could have been hurt feelings, tears, or silence. We hugged and kissed and let it go. We each had handled our earlier marriages so differently. Now, instead of conflict, silence and estrangement, we used understanding, warmth, and embraces.

CHAPTER 30

FIRST ANNIVERSARY

"Grow old with me; the best is yet to be.
The last of life,
For which the first was made."
—Robert Browning

December 7, 2014. We shared a champagne breakfast on the balcony of our stateroom. We munched on quiche, juicy strawberries, bright green kiwis, and warm croissants, the sweetness relieved with coffee. We were on board the Coral Princess, cruising the Panama Canal. We enjoyed our anniversary breakfast as we waited for the water to lower and enter the next lock. It was a party-like atmosphere. Passengers leaned out and waved homemade signs at the photographers on the dock while the ship was pulled by "mule" trains to the next lock. One hundred years ago, there were real mules pulling the ships.

I was celebrating my "third first anniversary." A waiter serenaded us with the song sung at our wedding, "You Lift Me Up." We thanked our Savior for bringing us together, two people who wanted to love again. It was a miracle.

My vows with each husband were "until death us do part." And death parted us. I didn't like it, didn't want it—but it had happened.

In the midst of this new joy, I had a powerful dream about Blair. He seemed far away, as if in another world. Rather than appearing as his friendly, loving self, he was withdrawn. I sensed that he wanted me to go with Jim.

Next morning, I tried to tell Jim about the dream. He nodded as he listened.

"Have you ever been so deep in trouble that you didn't think you could handle it?" Jim asked as he carefully took a sip of coffee. He looked at me with understanding in his eyes. This was the kind of question we often pondered.

I thought for a moment. "I've felt very overwhelmed." I talked about the times when Bill was so sick and about Blair's sudden death. Jim had listened to my stories many times but didn't mind hearing them again. I listened to his stories, too. As I thought about those hard moments, I began to weep—rare, hard chest sobs. I wasn't weeping because I missed my loved ones, who I knew were with our Savior. I was remembering the pain and helplessness, able to do nothing but wait for God's healing.

Jim knew what had precipitated my sobs. He'd been there too.

CHAPTER 31

DISNEYLAND IN A WHEELCHAIR AND OTHER ADVENTURES

*"Enter a magical kingdom where you can sail with
pirates . . . The happiest place on Earth!"*
—Disneyland Brochure

I'd had a wonderful birthday week. We had celebrated a day early so I could share the festivities with Annabel. I loved that my granddaughter and I shared birthdays only five days apart. Erika's family and a few extra guests helped to make the party special. It was Cinco de Mayo so we enjoyed a full Mexican menu with all the trimmings. As the family sang "Happy Birthday," Annabel and I leaned forward to blow out the candles on our chocolate cake.

We had so much to look forward to in the coming year, including a family trip to Disneyland in two weeks. I was grateful our families seemed to blend so well. Jim loved my family—and I loved his.

The next day Jim and I headed for the beach with his sister and brother-in-law, Ron and Rosaleen. Saturday dawned with clear blue skies. We ate our breakfast outside. The smell of frying bacon filled the campground and smoke from wood fires lazily wafted skyward. Later that afternoon, we set out on the beautiful Cape Lookout Trail. It was my first hike since foot surgery. At the final rocky outpost, the curve of the earth seemed visible. We returned to camp, invigorated but tired.

"Let's have a seafood meal tonight," Ron said. "I'll do the cooking." At a seafood market that guaranteed "freshly caught" varieties—pricey, but mouth-watering—we chose just-shucked oysters, fresh crab, salmon, and my favorite: scallops. Cooking on a camp stove made it necessary to eat our dinner in courses. We started with lightly-fried oysters and baguettes slathered in butter.

"This is delicious!" Jim and I declared as we sat by the warm campfire. We talked non-stop with Ron and Rosaleen about all kinds of things. Our kids. Current events. And then, we talked about marriage.

"We've really only had one argument since we've been married," Jim said.

"Go on, that can't be true!" countered Rosaleen, who was a marriage therapist. "You are still on the drugs of being newlyweds."

"Well, you might be right . . ." Jim said.

I remembered our recent argument over the stuffed green peppers. "Let me get that story," I said, jumping up to retrieve my manuscript from the RV at our campsite.

I opened the door and took a step up. *Don't forget the cat. She mustn't get out,* I reminded myself. Our cat sat looking at me from her perch on the high bed. I took the next step, fell backwards, and hit the ground three feet below.

Oh, no, was my first thought. *I won't be able to hike again!* Then came tremendous pain. I looked at my left ankle and saw it was bent in an abnormal angle.

"Jim!" I cried out. No response. "Jim!" I called again. Two women walking by the campsite asked if they could help. "Ask my husband to come over," I pleaded. Moments later, Jim stood by my side along with Ron and Rosaleen. "I did it this time," I moaned.

"Oh, honey," Jim said. He knelt behind me, holding me up. My foot flopped crookedly and I was afraid to move it. Rosaleen quickly found ice to place on the injury.

A park ranger cautioned us, "Tillamook Hospital is about ten miles away. You should have your foot checked."

I leaned back against Jim's chest. My head was whirling and I told myself, *Hold on. Don't black out.* I was going into shock and I knew that would make it worse. After a quick decision, Ron brought his truck over to our campsite and they carefully loaded me into the cab with my foot propped up, wrapped in a towel and ice.

After viewing the X-rays, the ER doctor told us surgery would be necessary. "You have an unsupported break and it will need hardware." I overheard the X-ray technician and nurse talking. In this small hospital, they had examined seven fractures that day. "I've been here for more than thirty years and I've *never* seen this many broken bones!" the X-ray tech declared. It reminded me how fragile we human beings are.

We discussed options: there was a competent orthopedic surgeon on staff, but no operating room available for two days. Several phone calls later, we decided to return to Vancouver, where a surgeon would perform surgery on my left ankle. I looked up at Jim, tears rolling down my cheeks. I was scared—and frustrated. I'd just finished being laid up with the surgery on my right foot, and now this! Jim hugged me and patted my hand. "It'll be all right. I love you. We'll get through this," he said.

"We need to stabilize your ankle and reposition the bones before you leave," the ER doctor said. She grasped my contorted ankle, and with a pop, the ankle was back in place. It was repositioned and splinted for the trip to the next hospital.

Somehow, Jim and the nurse helped me into the RV and up onto the four-foot high bed. The RV van rumbled on in the darkness. The two-hour trip seemed to take forever. I lay twenty feet behind the driver's seat and could hear the occasional *prrrp, prrrp, prrrp* of our tires hitting the traffic buttons on the lane markers. "Are you awake up there?" I called worriedly. I was scared Jim would fall asleep and we'd crash with my already-injured body.

"I'm wide awake and full of adrenaline. I won't fall asleep!"

At the hospital, Dr. Coale proposed a plan. "Your ankle won't be able to bear any weight for at least six weeks," he said.

"Do whatever needs to be done," Jim responded. "My wife is an active woman."

After the surgery, Dr. Coale told Jim that because of my osteoporosis, the break had looked like a fall from a tall building. "We put her ankle back together," he reported. "We used seven screws, one plate, and several pins."

A few hours later, I was back in my room, pain free. The anesthetic wouldn't wear off for hours. Both Jim and I were ready for sleep and it came easily, he lying in the cot beside me.

When I awoke the next morning, pain reared its fierce head. It was unexpectedly more intense than the foot surgery I'd had months before.

Two days later, I was back home. As I sat in the recliner, I told myself this wasn't a surprise to God. He knew before it ever happened that there would be no surgeon available in the small hospital at Tillamook. He knew the perfect physician—as it turned out, a specialist and nationally recognized vascular surgeon—who could put my ankle back together.

I was groggy with pain meds and limited to a walker and a wheelchair. Jim had his hands full. Friends brought meals, loaned crutches, and commiserated.

Our trip to Disneyland was to take place in two weeks. Would I be able to do it? I wasn't sure. It took every ounce of energy I had to go to the bathroom in the walker and my hop-scoot routine was exhausting. *How do elderly people do this*? I wondered. I huffed and puffed to accomplish minimal personal hygiene, brushing my teeth and hair and showering with help from Jim. Nothing was easy.

"Let's take it a day at a time," Jim said. "We'll decide just before if we can go."

Three days before our planned departure date, we decided I could do it. During our vacation, I discovered that sitting in a wheelchair was just as tiring as walking—maybe more so. I now look at people in wheelchairs much differently than before. Because you're not at eye level, you are ignored. It can be painful not to be seen.

Children, though, are the perfect height to meet you eye-to-eye. Interacting with them is delightful. I made a funny face at a little boy in a stroller who laughed gleefully. As we passed I waved goodbye and he waved back. And adults in wheelchairs share a silent communication. I made eye contact with a tough tattooed guy who tenderly held his toddler's hand.

In spite of my limitations, we had a great time in the world-famous amusement park. Each grandkid helped to push my wheelchair and I even went on some rides—wheelchairs take first priority, an advantage I hadn't counted on!

Seven weeks after my surgery, I became more independent, using a knee scooter to move around. Simple household tasks—such as watering plants, cooking meals, or shopping—remained a challenge. By the end of each day, I grew tired and frustrated that I couldn't do things as quickly as before my accident. Navigating carefully through the house and yard was tiresome but I reminded myself that some are bound to wheelchairs for the entirety of their lives.

In week ten, I began walking with a boot cast and crutch.

I was grateful for Jim, my husband of eighteen months, and his patient ways with me. I appreciated each grandchild who willingly pushed my chair or ran to fetch things for me. There was my extended family who prayed for me and cheered me on.

As the Apostle Paul said in Philippians 4:11, "I have learned to be content whatever the circumstances." That is my goal.

At Disneyland (Pictured: Top L-R: Caleb, Trent, Andrew, Erika, Jim; Bottom: L-R: Emily, Annabel, Shirley)

CHAPTER 32

GRIEVING LIFE

After we'd been married ten months, Jim and I went to a couples retreat. It was our first marriage seminar. We didn't think we needed marital advice, but we thought it would be fun to meet other couples at the beach setting. "I wonder if we'll be the *oldest* couple married the *least* amount of time," I joked. As it turned out, we enjoyed the companionship of couples of all ages.

Sitting in our beachfront room one evening, I reflected.

"You're awfully quiet. Whatcha thinking?" Jim asked, tipping his head toward me.

"I'm sad. There were so many things I could have done differently when Bill and I were together." I brushed a few tears away.

"How?" Jim touched my arm in sympathy, waiting for my reply.

"Well, now I realize that Bill's core personality traits were much different than mine. Remember what our seminar leader, Roger, told us? There are the Chargers, the Outgoing, the Responsible, and the Easygoing. I wish I'd understood these things earlier. Maybe our marriage would have been more harmonious . . ."

I pondered those lost years, grieving what we missed out on. "We wasted a lot of time. I just wish it would have been better."

"What's in the past can be like that. Grief, too," Jim said.

"Remember what the leader said in the last session? 'We're grieving life'? That helped me understand why sometimes I feel sad for what seems like no reason!"

We came to realize that Bill, Blair, and Kathy weren't struggling with past mistakes anymore. Jim and I were reaping the benefits of the challenges and trials of our previous marriages—and the brokenness. Ours would be better because of those trials. We were standing on the shoulders of our late spouses. And they were cheering us on in Heaven.

CHAPTER 33

GOD IS ALWAYS FAITHFUL

"Great is Thy Faithfulness, O God My Father,
There is no shadow of turning with Thee; Thou
changest Not, Thy compassions they fail not As
Thou hast been, Thou forever wilt be."
—Thomas O. Chisholm

Each morning, Jim and I have our talks. I am grateful to God for this man of my dreams, who listens patiently to my every word. We jokingly say our marriage is full of experience—more than eighty years of it. How long will we have together? I don't know. Our life together is still in the honeymoon stage. Marriage specialists say most couples have a year to eighteen months of the "happy drugs" before the realities of life take over. Yet even if those drugs of first love wear off, we will have a solid, beautiful love that endures during both the good and tough times. Perfection can only be in Heaven—but we are enjoying our Heaven on Earth.

When I was in my early teens, I loved to wander in a cemetery near my home in Brush Prairie. I enjoyed the sun-dappled place where I could read the names on tipped headstones more than a hundred years old. I wondered who these people were and what their lives had been like. On Father's Day this year, Jim and I stopped by this cemetery to remember some special people.

First we stopped at Bill's grave. I reflected on that man, gone nine years now. I traced my fingers over the words. *An Extravagant Gesture of the Creator.* "I wish I could have known him," Jim said.

"You will, one day," I reminded.

I looked at Carrie's headstone next. *Safe in the Arms of Jesus.*

We walked north toward my parents' gravesite. Dad's headstone said, *He Preached the Word.* Mom's said, *She Taught the Word.* I am grateful to my parents and their diligence to teach their children and others to love and follow Jesus Christ. Their lives were an example in which I never observed hypocrisy.

Writing my story, I've thought a lot about my parents and my past. How tenuous life is—even if we live to our nineties, as my mother did.

I don't know the future but I know I can trust my Savior. He brought me through the very hard times I've experienced.

God is with me in the joyful times too. He is with me when I celebrate birthdays or anniversaries, when I travel with my Jim, when we have new adventures, and when we make love.

There are nigglings of fear that creep into my thoughts. What if Jim dies? Can I make it without his love and care?

We pray that God will grant us many years together but we know that our lives are truly in His hands, not ours. We can trust in the God who loves us more than we love each other or ourselves.

So we do just that. We trust.

And He'll be there when He takes each of us home to Him.

He did it for me—Shirley. Shirley Quiring Rudberg Graybill Mozena.

And He'll do it for you, too. You need only ask Him.

GLOSSARY OF FAMILY MEMBERS

Jim P. Mozena and Shirley M. Graybill
married December 7, 2013

Shirley's Family:

Parents: Henry C. Quiring, September 11, 1917 - July 19, 1991
Rose Ann Richert Quiring, October 3, 1917 - November 12, 2010
Married October 3, 1937

> **Children:**
> Joyce Quiring Erickson, June 7, 1939
> Roger Dale Quiring, September 17, 1942
> Shirley Mae Quiring (Rudberg) (Graybill) Mozena, May 6, 1946
> Eileen Joy Quiring (Qutub), March 2, 1948
> Elizabeth Rose Quiring Berry, July 16, 1953

Shirley married Bill Rudberg on July 16, 1965
George William Rudberg, Jr: September 26, 1943 - February 3, 2006

Shirley married Blair Graybill on August 16, 2008
Henry Blair Graybill II: November 12, 1944 - January 31, 2010

Shirley's Children:

Todd William Rudberg, October 5, 1967
>> Rebekah, June 27, 1992
>> Sarah, October 9, 1996

Erika Ann Rudberg Sagert, June 27, 1973, married Trent Sagert in 1995
>> Andrew, June 10, 1999
>> Caleb, November 21, 2000
>> Annabel, May 1, 2004
>> Emily, September 30, 2005

Carrie Lynn Rudberg, June 13, 1977, stillborn

Stepsons:

Gregory Graybill, June 28, 1975, married Catherine Hunt in 2005
>> Meghan, June 28, 2012

Jonathan Graybill, January 30, 1978

Jim's Family:

James P. Mozena, August 4, 1949
Jim married Margaret Siberz March 22, 1969
Jim married Kathy Epperson October 22, 1983
>> Kathleen Sherman Epperson Mozena: December 18, 1946 - July 25, 2011

Jim's Children:

Vicki Lynn Mozena Campbell, August 19, 1969, married Chris Campbell in 1990
>> Taylor, April 11, 1992
>> Tucker, July 19, 1994
>> Kennedy August 19, 1996

Kevin Iner Mozena, April 22, 1973, married Kerri Diess in 2002
>> Rowan, May 14, 2007

Bryan James Mozena, married Kryston Shinn in 1997
     Austyn, March 3, 1998
     Haley, December 16, 2002

Stepson:
Ryan Epperson, married Jennifer Sizemore in 1992
     Landon, August 29, 2004
     Olivia, May 6, 2007

Stepdaughter:
Kara Epperson McKinney, July 10, 1976 - October 27, 2007,
  married Aaron McKinney in 2002
     Cole, March 4, 2005

ENDNOTES

1. Job 9:10
2. *The Christian's Secret of a Happy Life:* Revised Edition. Copyright 1888 Hannah Tatum Whitall Smith.
3. *Getting to the Other Side of Grief: Overcoming the Loss of a Spouse,* Susan J Zonnebelt-Smeenge and Robert C. DeVries. Baker Books, 1998.
4. Wright, H. Norman, Harvest House Publishers, 2009.
5. *Streams in the Desert 366 Daily Devotional Readings,* Cowman, L.B., Zondervan, 1997.
6. *Your Heritage: How to Be Intentional about the Legacy You Leave, J. Otis Ledbetter and Kurt Bruner. Victor Books, 1996.*
7. Harry D. Clarke (Used with permission, Hope Publishing Company).
8. Text: Fanny J. Crosby, Music: Phoebe P Knapp. Word Music, 1988.
9. Charles Wesley, from "Lyra Davidica."
10. Charlotte Elliott, William Bradbury.
11. Jeremiah E. Rankin.
12. Psalm 139:1-2.
13. Romans 8:35, 38-39
14. 2 Samuel 12:23 (TEV)

15. Luke 18:16
16. II Timothy 1:7
17. *Grieving the Loss of Someone You Love*, Lynn Brookside, Raymond R. Mitsch, Servant Publications, 1993.

Other Books by Shirley

Second Chances at Life and Love, with Hope

When Shirley and Bill set out on a dream trip in the beautiful northwest wilderness to celebrate their 40th anniversary, what develops is a nightmare that has no end. Mysterious pangs turn into a vicious virus that makes its way into Bill's body. Shirley finds comfort through her Savior during the six months of Bill's illness—an illness which eventually takes his life.

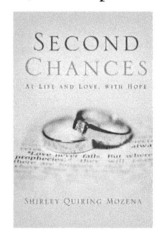

After a time, Shirley's heart aches for companionship. Little does she know that living a few miles from her home, a widower mourns the loss of his wife of 32 years. They meet and fall hopelessly in love, and their love takes them on a two-year journey of joy and adventure until once again overwhelming heartbreak rocks Shirley's world. This is a story of faith and courtship to strengthen your own soul.

Praise for Second Chances:

This story is wonderfully written with honesty and the depth of understanding that only grief can bring.In spite of the sad story of loss, the message of the book is one of joy in the goodness of today and hope for a future with God.

—Jan Pierce, author

Be ready for an "all-nighter" once you open this book. Shirley shares her times of love, sorrow, joy, peace and renewal. Shirley's willingness to open her heart to help others is seen throughout the book.

—Judi Mayfield, author

I just finished reading Second Chances. Thank you for sharing your story with authenticity and candor... your trust in our kind Father has been your bedrock...

—Diane Stevens

Second Chance at Love:
A Practical Guide to Remarriage after Loss

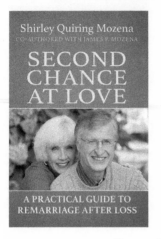

Whether your marriage was blissful or challenging, lengthy or short, it didn't end the way you imagined. Regardless of how you found yourself without a life partner, you may be at a point where you'd like to experience the love of a spouse again. Authors Shirley and Jim Mozena experienced devastating losses and then struggles in their relationships before finding renewed love with each other, and in Second Chance at Love they offer their insights to these difficult questions:

- Are you really ready?
- Is now the time?
- How do you know if you've found the right one?
- Is the potential pain of losing another spouse worth it?

The authors approach their answers with practical reality and their own vulnerability. They share the experiences of their first marriages, their second marriages, their journeys through what seemed like devastating losses, and the gifts of finding love and another chance to share their lives with a spouse after death and divorce.

In addition to the down-to-earth guidance on the situations you face when considering marrying again, Shirley and Jim have created valuable questionnaires to identify issues and facilitate discussions with potential mates. The information contained in this book will give you confidence and peace as you navigate these hopeful waters.

Second Chance at Love: A Practical Guide to Remarriage after Loss
is available at Shirley's website (shirleymozena.com)
or on amazon.com and barnesandnoble.com

Order Information

To order additional copies of this book or any of Shirley's
books, please visit www.shirleymozena.com.
Also available on Amazon.com and BarnesandNoble.com.